Web Engineering

M.Sc Computer Science

IIIrd Semester

University of Calicut

Edited by

Dr. Mini. T.V.

Fancy Joy

Published by

BONFRING®
Intellectual Integrity

Web Engineering

ISBN 978-93-86638-52-6

Edited by

Dr. Mini.T.V.
Fancy Joy

Bonfring
309, 2nd Floor, 5th Street Extension, Gandhipuram,
Coimbatore-641 012.
Tamilnadu, India.
E-mail: info@bonfring.org
Website: www.bonfring.org
Phone: 0422 4213231

Preface

The importance of **Web Engineering** is well known in various engineering fields. The book uses plain, lucid language to explain fundamental of this subject. This book provides logical method of explaining various complicated concepts and stepwise methods to explain the important topics.

All care has been take care to make students comfortable in understanding the basic concepts of the subject.

We wish to express our thanks to all those who helped in making this book a reality.

We wish to thank the publisher and the entire team who have taken immense pain to get this book in time with quality printing.

Dr. Mini.T.V.
Fancy Joy

Syllabus

CSS3E05f | Web Engineering

Unit I

Web Engineering (WE) – introduction – motivation – categories & characteristics of web applications – product related, usage related and development related –evolution of WE.

Unit II

Requirements Engineering (RE) for web applications – introduction – fundamentals –sources of requirements – RE activities – RE specifications in WE - RE principles for web applications – adapting RE methods for web applications development –requirement types, notations, tools.

Unit III

Web application architecture – introduction – fundamentals – definition of architecture – developing and characterizing architectures – components of a generic web application architecture – layered architecture – database centric architecture - architecture for web document management – architecture for multimedia data.

Unit IV

Modeling web applications – introduction – modeling specifics in WE – levels – aspects – phases of customizations – modeling requirements – hypertext modeling - hypertext structure modeling concepts – access modeling concepts. Web application design – web design from an evolutionary perspective – information design –software design – merging information design & software design – problems and restrictions in integrated web design – a proposed structural approach – presentation design – presentation of nodes and meshes – device independent development – approaches – interaction design – user interaction – user interface organization – navigation design – deigning a link representation – designing link internals – navigation and orientation – structural dialog for complex activities –interplay with technology and architecture – functional design.

Unit V

Testing web applications – introduction – fundamentals – terminology – quality characteristics – test objectives – test levels – role of tester – test specifics in we – test approaches – conventional, agile - test schemes – three test dimensions – applying the scheme to web applications – test methods and techniques – link testing – browser testing – usability testing – load, stress and continues testing –testing security – test-driven development. Web project development – scope – refining frame work activities – building an WebE team - risk management – making schedule – managing quality, change – project tracking.

<table>
<tr><th>Chapter</th><th>Contents</th><th>Page No</th></tr>
</table>

CHAPTER I

AN INTRODUCTION TO WEB ENGINEERING

Modern Web applications are full-fledged, complex software systems. Therefore, the development of Web applications requires a methodologically sound engineering approach. Based on Software Engineering, Web Engineering comprises the use of systematic and quantifiable approaches in order to accomplish the specification, implementation, operation, and maintenance of high-quality Web applications. We distinguish Web applications from the viewpoints of development history and complexity: Web applications can have document centric, interactive, transactional, or ubiquitous characteristics, or even features of the semantic Web. The particular requirements of Web Engineering result from the special characteristics of Web applications in the areas of the software product itself, its development, and its use. Evolution is a characteristic that encompasses these three areas.

1.1. Motivation

The World Wide Web has a massive and permanent influence on our lives. Economy, industry, education, healthcare, public administration, entertainment – there is hardly any part of our daily lives that has not been pervaded by the World Wide Web, or Web for short (Ginige and Murugesan 2001b). The reason for this omnipresence lies especially in the very nature of the Web, which is characterized by global and permanent availability and comfortable and uniform access to often widely distributed information producible by anyone in the form of Web pages (Berners-Lee 1996, Murugesan et al. 1999). Most probably you came across this book by entering the term "Web Engineering" into a search engine. Then, you might have used a portal for comparing offers of different vendors and finally, you may have bought the book using an online shop.

While originally the Web was designed as a purely informational medium, it is now increasingly evolving into an application medium (Ginige and Murugesan 2001a, Murugesan et al. 1999). Web applications today are full-fledged, complex software systems providing interactive, data intensive, and customizable services accessible through different devices; they provide a facility for the realization of user transactions and usually store data in an underlying database (Kappel et al. 2002). The distinguishing feature of Web applications compared with traditional software applications is the way in which the Web is used, i.e. its technologies and standards are used as a development platform and as a user platform at the same time. A Web application can therefore be defined as follows:

> A Web application is a software system based on technologies and standards of the World Wide Web Consortium (W3C) that provides Web specific resources such as content and services through a user interface, the Web browser.

This definition explicitly includes technologies as well as user interaction. From this we can conclude that technologies on their own, such as Web services, are not Web applications, but they can be part of one. Furthermore, this definition implies that Web sites without software components, such as static HTML pages, are not Web applications either. Of course broader definitions are conceivable that might include Web services and Web sites (Baresi et al. 2000). The conclusions of this book can be applied analogously for these cases as well. "Limiting" the definition to software intensive and interactive Web applications, however, actually increases the scope of the problem, as both the software and the user interface aspects in relation to the Web have to be examined, which is one of the objectives of this book.

Despite the fundamental changes in the orientation of the Web from an informational to an application medium, the current situation of ad hoc development of Web applications reminds us of the software development practices of the 1960s, before it was realized that the development of applications required more than programming expertise (Murugesan 2000, Pressman 2000a, Retschitzegger and Schwinger 2000). The development of Web applications is often seen as a one-time event, it is often spontaneous, usually based on the knowledge, experiences, and development practices of individual developers, limited to reuse in the sense of the "Copy&Paste paradigm", and ultimately characterized by inadequate documentation of design decisions. Although this procedure may appear pragmatic, such quick and dirty development methods often result in massive quality problems and consequently in great problems in operation and maintenance. The applications developed are often heavily technology dependent and error-prone, characterized by a lack of performance, reliability, and scalability, user-friendliness, and therefore also acceptance (Fraternali 1999). The strong interlinking of Web applications additionally increases the danger of problems spreading from one application to the other. The reasons for this situation are complex (cf. e.g. Balasubramaniam et al. 2002, Ginige 2000, Lowe 1999, Murugesan 2000, Murugesan and Ginige 2005, Rosson et al. 2005):

- *Document-centric approach*: The development of Web applications is often still considered to be document centric, i.e. an authoring activity that includes the creation and linking of Web sites and the inclusion of graphics (Ginige et al. 1995). Even though some types of Web applications (e.g. homepages, online newspapers, etc.) fall in this category, an authoring viewpoint is not adequate for the development of software intensive Web applications.

- *The assumed simplicity of Web applications development*: The broad availability of different tools, such as HTML editors or form generators (cf. Fraternali 1999) permits the creation of simple Web applications without specialized knowledge. Usually the emphasis is on visual design rather than internal structuring and programming. This results in inconsistencies and redundancy.

- *Know-how from relevant disciplines cannot be applied or is not used*: It is a common misconception that the development of Web applications is analogous to the development of traditional applications and that therefore the methods of Software Engineering can be used in the sense of a systematic, disciplined approach with adequate quality control measures. This, however, appears inadequate in many cases due to the special characteristics of Web applications (cf. Section 1.3). Additionally, concepts and techniques from relevant areas, such as hypertext or human-computer interaction, are often not applied in a consequent manner (Deshpande et al. 1999). Development standards for high-quality Web applications are nonexistent – this is in part due to the relatively short history of the Web.

The current practice in Web application development and the increasing complexity and relevance of Web applications for many areas of our society, in particular for the efficient hand-ling of critical business processes (e.g. in e-commerce) (Deshpande and Hansen 2001), give growing cause for concern about this type of development and the long-term quality of Web applications, which already form the largest share of the individual software developed today. A survey by the Cutter Consortium (Cutter Consortium 2000) found that the top problem areas of large-scale Web application projects were the failure to meet business needs (84%), project schedule delays (79%), budget overrun (63%), lack of functionality (53%), and poor quality of deliverables (52%). Consequently, one could speak of a new form of software crisis (Naur and Randell 1968) – the *Web crisis* (Ginige and Murugesan 2001a). Due to the omnipresence of Web applications and their strong cross-dependency, this Web crisis could be considerably more serious and widespread than the software crisis of the 1960s (Murugesan 2000, Lowe and Hall 1999, Retschitzegger et al. 2002). This is the challenge Web Engineering seeks to address. Web Engineering is not a one-time event; rather it is a process performed throughout the whole lifecycle of a Web application, similar to Software Engineering. In which ways does Web Engineering differ from Software Engineering and is it justifiable to consider it a separate discipline?

A discipline can be defined as a field of study, i.e. a more or less self-contained field of science including research, teaching, and well-established scientific knowledge in the form of publications. The large number of publications, lectures, emerging curricula, workshops, and conferences[1] show that according to this definition, Web Engineering can be considered an independent branch of Software Engineering (Kappel et al. 2005). *Engineering* in general means the practical application of science to commerce or industry with the goal of designing applications in a better, i.e. faster/cheaper/more secure/etc., way than hitherto. *Software Engineering* is defined as *the application of science and mathematics by which the capabilities of computer equipment are made useful to man via computer programs, procedures, and associated documentation* (Boehm 1976). Based on this definition and on (Deshpande et al. 2002) we define Web Engineering as follows:

> 1) Web Engineering is the application of systematic and quantifiable approaches (concepts, methods, techniques, tools) to cost-effective requirements analysis, design, implementation, testing, operation, and maintenance of high-quality Web applications.
>
> 2) Web Engineering is also the scientific discipline concerned with the study of these approaches.

Related terms in the literature coined for similar topics are e.g. *Web Site Engineering* (Powell et al. 1998, Schwickert 1997), *Hypermedia Engineering* (Lowe and Hall 1999), *Document Engineering* (Glushko and McGrath 2002), *Content Engineering* (Reich and Guntner¨ 2005), and *Internet Software Engineering* (Balasubramaniam et al. 2002). In comparison, "Web Engineering" is a concise term, although strictly speaking not completely accurate – it is not the Web that is engineered, but rather Web applications. But "Web Applications Engineering" does not quite have the same ring to it.

From the point of view of Software Engineering, the development of Web applications is a new application domain (Glass 2003, Kautz and Nørbjerg 2003). Despite some similarities to traditional applications, the special characteristics of Web applications require an adaptation of many Software Engineering approaches or even the development of completely new approaches (Deshpande et al. 1999, Murugesan et al. 1999).

The basic principles of Web Engineering can, however, be described similarly to those of Software Engineering (cf. e.g. Lowe 1999, Selmi 2005):

- Clearly defined goals and requirements.
- Systematic development of a Web application in phases.
- Careful planning of these phases.
- Continuous audit of the entire development process.

Web Engineering makes it possible to plan and iterate development processes and thus also facilitates the continuous evolution of Web applications. This permits not only cost reduction and risk minimization during development and maintenance, but also an increase in quality, as well as measurement of the quality of the results of each phase (Ginige and Murugesan 2001b, Mendes and Mosley 2006).

The structure of this book is based on that of the *Guide to the Software Engineering Body of Knowledge* (SWEBOK, Bourque and Dupuis 2005), i.e. the individual chapters follow the structuring of traditional Software Engineering. Each of the contributions focuses on the special characteristics of the relevant topic in relation to the Web. The following section defines the categories of Web applications. Section 1.3 expands on this by describing the special characteristics of Web applications. Finally, section 1.4 presents an overview of the structure of the book.

1.2.   Categories of Web Applications

Web applications have varying degrees of complexity. They may be purely informational or handle full-size/full-fledged 24/7 e-commerce applications. Fig. 1-1 identifies different categories of Web applications depending on their *development history* and their *degree of complexity* and gives examples (cf. Murugesan 2000).[2] We must bear in mind that there is a correlation between the chronology of development and complexity. Workflow-based applications, for example, are transaction-based, i.e. the higher level of development requires the previous development of a less complex category. However, there may be exceptions to that rule in that some of the categories (e.g. the portal-oriented applications) are historically rather recent while having a lower degree of complexity.

Web presences of organizations that have been on the Web since the beginning often have a development history similar to the one described in Fig. 1-1. Of course, the development of a Web application can be started in any of these categories and later expanded to increasing degrees of complexity. Newer categories are generally more complex, but this does not mean they can fully replace the older generation. Each of these categories has its own specific fields of application. In consequence, complex Web applications in particular can typically be assigned to several categories at once. Online shopping malls for example not only integrate different service providers but also offer several search options, order status monitoring, and in some cases even online auctions.

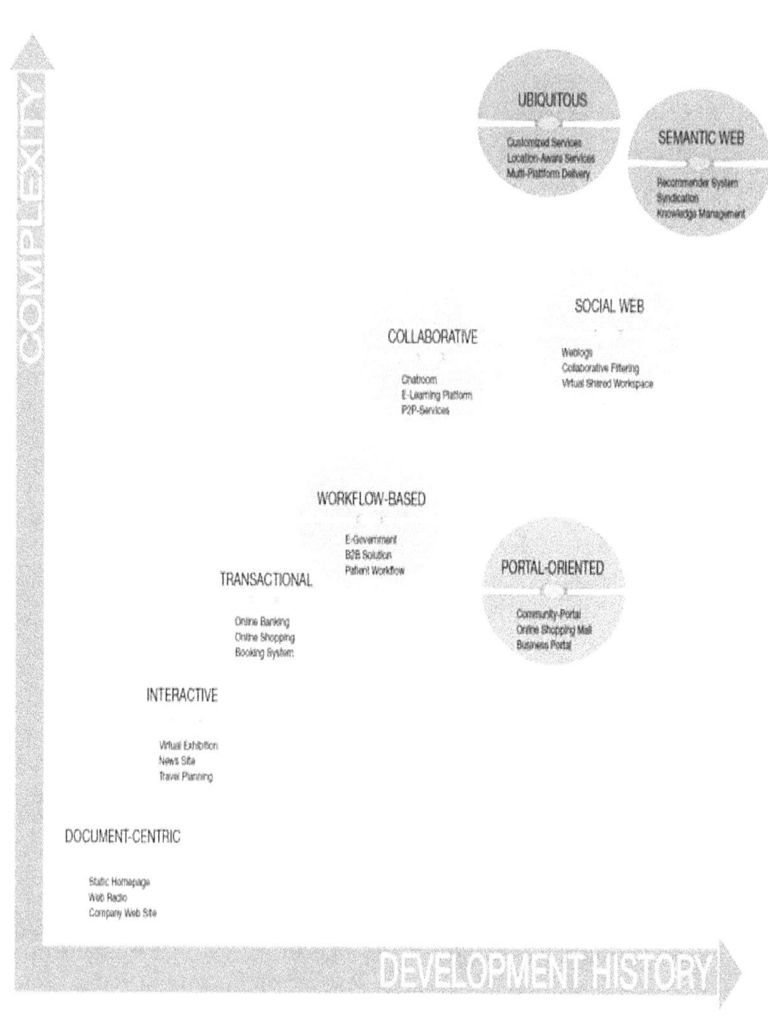

Figure 1.1: Categories of Web Applications

We also see that the different categories of Web applications cover many traditional fields of application, such as online banking, but that at the same time completely new fields of application are created, such as location-aware services. We will now describe the relevant features of these categories.

Document centric Web sites are the precursor to Web applications. Web pages are stored on a Web server as ready-made, i.e. static, HTML documents and sent to the Web client in response to a request. These Web pages are usually updated manually using respective tools. Especially for Web sites requiring frequent changes or for sites with huge numbers of pages this is a significant cost factor and often results in outdated information. Additionally, there is a danger of inconsistencies, as some content is frequently represented redundantly on several Web pages for easy access. The main benefits are the simplicity and stability of such Web sites and the short response time, as the pages are already stored on the Web server. Static homepages, webcasts, and simple web presences for small businesses belong in this category.

With the introduction of the Common Gateway Interface (http://hoohoo.ncsa.uiuc.edu/ cgi/interface.html) and HTML forms, *interactive Web applications* emerged, offering a first, simple, form of interactivity by means of forms, radio buttons and selection menus. Web pages and links to other pages are generated dynamically according to user input. Examples for this category are virtual exhibitions, news sites, or timetable information.

Transactional Web applications were created to provide more interactivity, giving the user the possibility of not only interacting with the application in a read-only manner, but also by performing updates on the underlying content. Considering a tourism information system this would allow, for example, to update the content in a decentralized way or make it possible to book rooms (cf. e.g. Proll̈ and Retschitzegger 2000). The prerequisite for this are database systems that allow efficient and consistent handling of the increasing amount of content in Web applications and offer the possibility of structured queries. Online banking, online shopping, and booking systems belong in this category.

Workflow-based Web applications allow the handling of workflows within or between different companies, public authorities, and private users. A driving force for this is the availability of appropriate Web services to guarantee interoperability (Weerawarana et al. 2005). The complexity of the services in question, the autonomy of the participating companies and the necessity for the workflows to be robust and flexible are the main challenges. Examples for this category are Business-to-Business solutions (B2B solutions) in e-commerce, e-government applications in the area of public administration, or Web-based support of patient workflows in the health sector.

Whereas workflow-based Web applications require a certain structuring of the automated processes and operations, *collaborative Web applications* are employed especially for cooperation purposes in unstructured operations (groupware). There the need for communication between the cooperating users is particularly high. Collaborative Web applications support shared information and workspaces (e.g. WikiWiki, http://c2.com/cgi/wiki, or BSCW, http://bscw.gmd.de/) in order to generate, edit, and manage shared information. They are also used to keep logs of many small entries and edits (as in Weblogs), to mediate meetings or make decisions (e.g. argumentation systems such as QuestMap (http://www.compendiuminstitute.org/) or simple chat rooms), as scheduling systems, or as e-learning platforms.

While originally the Web was characterized by anonymity, there is an increasing trend towards a *social Web*, where people provide their identity to a (small) community of others with similar interests. Weblogs or collaborative filtering systems such as (http://friendster.com) for instance, which serve the purpose of not only finding related objects of interest but also finding people with similar interests, belong to that category of applications.

Portal-oriented Web applications provide a single point of access to separate, potentially heterogeneous sources of information and services (Wege 2002). Makers of browsers, such as Microsoft and Netscape, search engines such as Yahoo, online services such as AOL, media conglomerates, and other companies have become aware of the demand for this and now offer central hubs, so-called portals, as a point of access to the Web. In addition to these general portals, there are various specialized portals such as business portals, marketplace portals in the form of online shopping malls, and community portals. Business portals give employees and/or business partners focused access to different sources of information and services through an intranet or extranet. Marketplace portals are divided into horizontal and vertical market places.

Horizontal marketplaces operate on the business-to-consumer market offering consumer goods directly to the general public, and in business-to-business, selling their products to companies from other sectors. Vertical marketplaces consist of companies from a single sector, e.g. suppliers on one side and manufacturing companies on the other. Community portals are directed at specific target groups, e.g. young people, and try to create customer loyalty through user interaction or to provide individual offers through appropriate user management (one-to-one marketing). The increasingly important category of *ubiquitous Web applications* provides customized services anytime anywhere and for any device, thus facilitating ubiquitous access. An example of this would be displaying the menu of the day on the mobile devices of all users entering a restaurant between 11 am and 2 pm.

For this type of system it is important to take into account the limitations of mobile devices (bandwidth, screen size, memory, immaturity of software, etc.) and the context in which the Web application is currently being used. Based on this dynamic adjustments according to the users' situation (Kappel et al. 2002) can be made. Currently existing Web applications of this type usually offer a very limited form of ubiquity only supporting one aspect–either personalization or location-aware services or multi-platform delivery (Kappel et al. 2003).

Current developments, however, especially the increasing convergence of the TIMES industry (Telecommunications, Information technology, Multimedia, Education and Entertainment, Security), will lead to a situation in the near future where ubiquitous applications will dominate the market. One of these developments is the *Semantic Web*. The goal of the Semantic Web is to present information on the Web not merely for humans, but also in a machine-readable form (Berners-Lee et al. 2001).

This would facilitate knowledge management on the Web, in particular the linking and reuse of knowledge (content syndication), as well as locating new relevant knowledge, e.g. by means of recommender systems.

Through increased interoperation on the semantic level and the possibility of automating tasks (via software agents), we believe the Web will become even more ubiquitous and therefore relevant for everyday life.

1.3. Characteristics of Web Applications

Web applications differ from traditional, non-Web-based applications in a variety of features worth looking into. These are characteristics that traditional applications lack completely (e.g. non-linear navigation) on the one hand and characteristics that are of particular importance in Web applications on the other hand (e.g. frequency of updates) (Balasubramaniam et al. 2002, McDonald and Welland 2001b, Whitehead 2002). Whether a certain characteristic is present and to what degree depends partly on the type of Web application: the development of transactional Web applications such as e-commerce systems requires greater focus on the content being up to date and consistent as compared with pure information provision systems – e.g. virtual exhibitions.

These characteristics are the reason why many concepts, methods, techniques, and tools of traditional Software Engineering have to be adapted to the needs of Web Engineering or may even be totally inadequate. Fig. 1-2 gives an overview of these characteristics and arranges them along the three dimensions: "product", "usage", and "development" with their "evolution" as an encompassing dimension.

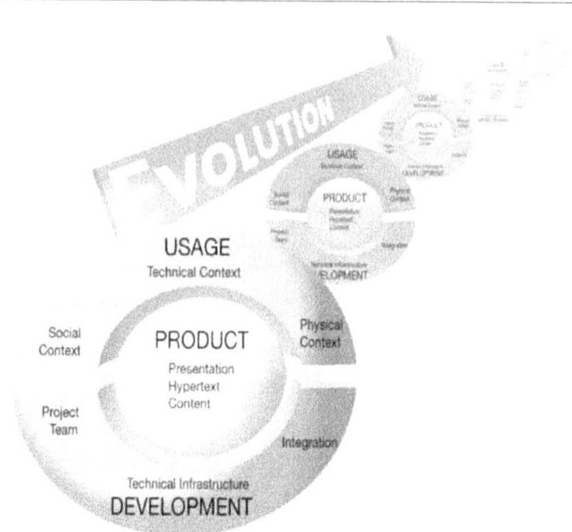

Figure 1.2: Dimensions According to ISO/IEC 9126-1 for the Categorization of Characteristics of Web Applications

These dimensions are based on the ISO/IEC 9126-1 standard for the evaluation of software quality characteristics (http://www.iso.org/). By assigning the different characteristics of Web applications to these dimensions we can also see their influence on the quality of applications and thus take the characteristics as a starting point for the definition of Web Engineering requirements (cf. Section 1.4). In addition to product-related, usage-related, and development-related characteristics, we have evolution as a fourth dimension governing the other three dimensions. Products must be adaptable, new contextual information should be considered during use, and development faces continually changing conditions, to name but a few examples. In the following, we will describe the individual characteristics according to these dimensions. References are made to those chapters of the book expanding on the characteristic in question. An overview of the influences of these characteristics and their occurrence in the chapters of this book is given in Table 1-1.

1.3.1. *Product-Related Characteristics*

Product-related characteristics constitute the major building blocks of a Web application, consisting of content, the hyper textual structure (navigational structure), and presentation (the user interface). Following the object-oriented paradigm, each of these parts has not only a structural or static aspect, but also a behavioral or dynamic aspect.

Table 1.1: Web Engineering Requirements

The table below relates the **Characteristics of Web Applications** (left) to the chapters of the book under **Web Engineering** (columns 2–14): 2. Requirements Engineering, 3. Modeling, 4. Architectures, 5. Technology Aware Design, 6. Technologies, 7. Testing, 8. Operation and Maintenance, 9. Project Management, 10. Development Process, 11. Usability, 12. Performance, 13. Security, 14. Semantic Web.

Category	Sub-context	Group	Characteristic	2	3	4	5	6	7	8	9	10	11	12	13	14
Product		content	document character / multimediality		x	x		x					x			
Product		content	quality aspects	x	x				x	x			x			
Product		hypertext	non-linearity		x		x		x				x	x		
Product		hypertext	disorientation / cognitive overload		x								x	x		
Product		presentation	aesthetics	x	x		x				x		x			
Product		presentation	self explication	x	x						x		x			
Usage	social context		spontaneity		x	x					x			x		
Usage	social context		multiculturalism	x	x					x			x	x		
Usage	technical context		quality of service	x	x				x				x	x		
Usage	technical context		multi-platform delivery	x	x	x	x	x	x				x	x		
Usage	natural context		globality		x	x			x						x	
Usage	natural context		availability		x				x			x				
Development	team		multidisciplinarity	x					x		x					x
Development	team		youthfulness						x		x					
Development	team		community development			x	x								x	x
Development	infrastructure		inhomogeneity		x	x	x	x	x				x			
Development	infrastructure		immaturity			x	x	x		x	x					
Development	process		flexibility	x					x		x	x				
Development	process		parallelism								x	x				
Development	integration		internal integration	x		x	x						x	x		
Development	integration		external integration	x		x	x					x	x			x
Evolution			continuous change	x		x			x	x			x	x		
Evolution			competitive pressure			x	x		x	x			x			
Evolution			short lifetime			x			x	x	x	x		x	x	

Content

Generating content, making it available, integrating, and updating it is equally important as the development and provision of the actual software of a Web application. Web applications are used expressly because of the content they offer – true to the motto "Content is King". Web application developers must therefore not only act as programmers but also as authors. Important aspects are the varying degree of structure of the content and the quality demands users make on the content.

- *Document-centric character and multimediality*: Depending on the structuring, content is provided as tables, text, graphics, animations, audio, or video. "Document character" in Web applications refers to the fact that content is provided, i.e. documents are generated that present information in an appropriate way for certain user groups (e.g., tourist information on a holiday region). This implies amongst others special requirements on usability. Content is in part also generated and updated dynamically; e.g. the number of available rooms in a tourism information system. Furthermore, the Web serves as an infrastructure for the transmission of multimedia content, e.g. in video conferences or Real Audio applications.

- *Quality demands*: Depending on the application area, the content of a Web application is not only subject to differing update frequencies, but also to different quality metrics regarding its being up to date, exact, consistent and reliable. This requires not only the consideration of these quality demands in the requirements definition but also the evaluation of compliance with these.

News sites, for instance, have a very high frequency of updates and face very high user demands regarding topicality.

The Web as a medium in its own right, alongside television, radio, and print media, offers great potential for addressing these demands better than traditional media, e.g. through personalization. On the other hand, there is a line of argumentation saying that "smart", i.e., location aware, personalized applications also require for new genres to be developed: the reason is that these new content-driven applications such as podcasting or mobile contents are such a different medium that one cannot simply adapt existing content but that rather new genres have to be developed in order to provide high quality of user perception (see also "Content Engineering" Reich and Guntner" 2005).

Particularly high quality is required for price and availability information in online-shopping systems, as they form the basis of the business transaction (cf. e.g. Proll" and Retschitzegger 2000).

Incorrect prices can lead to a cancellation of the sale, out-of-date information on availability can result in products on stock not being sold or in delivery problems because products listed as available are not on stock after all.

Regardless of where a Web application is used, content quality is a critical factor for its acceptance. The great challenge is being able to guarantee the quality of the data despite the large volume and high frequency of updates.

Hypertext

Amongst the specific characteristics of Web applications is the non-linear nature of hypertextual documents (Conklin 1987). The hypertext paradigm as a basis for the structuring and presentation of information was first mentioned by Vannevar Bush (Bush 1945). There are many different hypertext models (McCarty 2003), and the Web itself defines a very simple model of its own. Basic elements of hypertext models are *nodes, links* and *anchors*. A node is a self-contained uniquely identifiable information unit. On the Web this might be an HTML document which can be reached via a URL (*Uniform Resource Locator*). A link is the path from one node to another. On the Web, these paths are always unidirectional and their meaning is not clearly defined. Possible meanings include "next node according to recommended reading order" or "diagram for mathematical formula". An anchor is the area within the content of a node that is the source or destination of a link, e.g. a sequence of words in a text or a graphical object in a drawing. On the Web, anchors are only possible in HTML documents.

The essential feature of the hypertext paradigm is the *non-linearity* of content production by the authors and of content reception by the users together with the potential problems of *disorientation* and *cognitive overload*.

- *Non-linearity*: Hypertexts imply stereotypes of relatively systematic reading, and in this, Web applications differ fundamentally from traditional software applications. We can distinguish among others between *browsing*, e.g. in online shopping applications, *queries*, e.g. in virtual exhibitions, and *guided tours*, e.g. in e-learning applications. This individual style of reading, adaptable to user needs and behavior, is ideally suited to the human learning ability. Users may move freely through the information space, depending on their interests and previous knowledge. Anchors (and, consequently, also links) are not only predefined statically by the authors, but are also generated dynamically (computed links) in a predefined reaction to user behavior patterns. Creating hypertext is always a challenge for the authors, as they seek to avoid disorientation and cognitive overload for the users.
- *Disorientation and cognitive overload*: It is particularly important in Web application development to cope with these two fundamental problems of the hypertext paradigm. Disorientation is the tendency to lose one's bearings in a non-linear document. Cognitive overload is caused by the additional concentration required to keep in mind several paths or tasks simultaneously. Sitemaps, key word searches, retracing of "paths" (*history mode*) and display of access time and time spent on the site help users

to keep their orientation within the application. Meaningful linking and intelligent link naming reduce cognitive overload (Conklin 1987). Additionally, design patterns in modeling the hypertext aspect may also help counteract this problem (Akanda and German 2005, German and Cowan 2000, Lyardet and Rossi 2001, Panagis et al. 2005) .

Presentation

Two special features of Web applications at the presentation level, i.e. the user interface, are aesthetics and self-explanation.

- *Aesthetics*: In contrast to traditional applications, the aesthetics of the presentation level of a Web application, the "look and feel" of the user interface, is a central factor not least because of the high competitive pressure on the Web. The visual presentation of Web pages is subject to fashion trends and often determines success or failure, in particular for e-commerce applications (Pressman 2005).
- *Self-explanation*: Besides aesthetics, it is essential that Web applications are self-explanatory, i.e. it should be possible to use a Web application without documentation. The navigation system or interaction behavior must be consistent within the whole application, so that users can quickly become familiar with the usage of the Web application.

1.3.2. Usage-Related Characteristics

Compared with traditional applications, the usage of Web applications is extremely hetero-geneous. Users vary in numbers and cultural background, devices have differing hardware and software characteristics, and the time and location from where the application is accessed cannot be predicted (Kappel et al. 2000).

Additionally, developers not only have no possibility of knowing the potential diversity of these so-called *contextual factors* in advance, they also cannot influence them in any way because of their autonomous nature. There is hardly any way of predicting for example the usage frequency for a given Web application.

The usage of Web applications is therefore characterized by the necessity to continuously adapt to specific usage situations, so-called *contexts*. Adjustment to these contexts can be equally necessary for all parts of the Web application, i.e. content, hypertext, and presentation. Because of the fundamental significance of adjustment to contexts, usage-related characteristics are divided into three groups: *social context*, *technical context*, and *natural context* (Kappel et al. 2000, Koch and Wirsing 2001, Kappel et al. 2003).

Social Context: Users

The social context refers to user-specific aspects; spontaneity and multiculturality in particular create a high degree of heterogeneity.

- *Spontaneity*: Users can visit a Web application whenever they want and leave it again – possibly for a competitor's site. The Web user cannot be expected to be loyal to any content provider. The Web is a medium that entails no obligation (Holck and Clemmensen 2002). Since it is easy to find competing applications with the help of search engines users will only use a Web application if it appears to bring them immediate advantage.

Spontaneity in use also means that the number of users cannot be reliably predicted as for traditional applications. Scalability, therefore, is extremely important (Hendrickson and Fowler 2002).

- *Multiculturality*: Web applications are developed for different user groups. If the group in question is a known user group, as would be the case with an intranet or extranet, this is largely comparable to traditional applications. When developing a Web application for an anonymous group of users, however, there will be large and hardly foreseeable heterogeneities in terms of abilities (e.g. disabilities), knowledge (e.g. application expertise), and preferences (e.g. interests) (Kobsa 2001). In order to allow appropriate customization, assumptions about the user contexts must be made at the development stage of a Web application. These will be taken into consideration when adapting the components of the application. Regular customers might be given special discounts (adaptation of content), new customers might receive a guided tour through the Web application (adaptation of hypertext), and users with visual impairments might be aided by appropriate font sizes (adaptation of presentation). Personalization often requires users to set their preferences (e.g. preferred payment method on http://www.amazon.com).

  The large variety of possible user groups also makes it hard to define a representative sample for a requirements analysis.

Technical Context: Network and Devices

The technical context comprises properties relating to the network connection concerning *quality of service*, and the hardware and software of the devices used to access the Web application, for *multi-platform delivery*.

- *Quality of service*: Technically, Web applications are based on the client/server principle. The characteristics of the transmission medium, such as bandwidth, reliability, and varying stability of the connection are independent factors that must be considered when developing a Web application to guarantee appropriate quality of service (Badrinath et al. 2000, Pressman 2005). For example, the parameter "maximum bandwidth" can be adjusted to optimize the amount of data transferred, so that multimedia content, e.g. videos, will be transferred with lower resolution in case of lower bandwidth. While for traditional applications the specifications of the network are usually known beforehand, Web application developers need to make assumptions about these properties. With the trend towards mobile Web applications, this is of increasing importance, as convergent networks require even more adaptation on the application level (Venkatakrishnan and Murugesan 2005).

- *Multi-platform delivery*: Web applications usually offer services not only to a specific type of device, but rather any, increasingly mobile, devices with very different specifications (e.g. monitor size, memory capacity, installed software) (Eisenstein et al. 2001). The large number of different browser versions is also a challenge, as they have different functionalities and restrictions (and also often do not implement the specifications as expected). This poses difficulties in creating a consistent user interface and in testing Web applications.

Additionally, users can configure browsers autonomously. Presentation (e.g. hide images), access rights (e.g. for Java applets), and range of functions (e.g. cookies and caching) can all be configured individually, thus having an influence on performance, transaction functionality, and possibilities of interaction, to name but a few.

Based on assumptions of typical classes of devices, Web application developers can adapt content to PDAs (*personal digital assistants*) by not transmitting images or videos (*web clipping*) and instead providing links or descriptive text. At the hypertext level, printer versions of hypertext documents can be provided. Finally, in order to account for different versions of JavaScript in different browsers, platform-independent libraries can be used in the development process (see e.g. http://www.domapi.com).

Natural Context: Location and Time

The natural context includes aspects of the location and time of access. Globality and availability create a high degree of heterogeneity.

- *Globality*: The location from which a Web application is accessed, e.g. the geographical position, is important for the internationalization of Web applications regarding regional, cultural and linguistic differences. Additionally, the (physical) location can be used in conjunction with location models to define a logical position such as place of residence or workplace in order to provide location-aware services. Location-awareness imposes further difficulties for the testing of Web applications as it is often hard to simulate changing locations and/or test all possible locations. Global availability also increases the demands on security of Web applications to prevent users from accessing – deliberately or by accident – private or confidential areas.

- *Availability*: The "instant delivery mechanism" inherent in the very nature of the Web makes the application immediately available. The Web application becomes instantly usable, which means that the quality of the developed product must be secured. Permanent availability 24/7 also increases the demands on the stability of Web applications . In addition, time-aware services are made possible through consideration of the time aspect (e.g. timetable information depending on the time of day and day of the week).

1.3.3. Development-Related Characteristics

The development of Web applications is characterized by the necessary resources, such as the *development team* and the *technical infrastructure*, the *development process* itself, and the necessary *integration* of already existing solutions.

The Development Team

The development of Web applications is strongly influenced by the fact that development teams are *multidisciplinary* and generally rather young. These factors and the methods of the so-called *community development* contribute to a completely new way of organizing collaboration of different groups of developers.

The different points of view and emphases must be brought together through appropriate project management and an adapted development process.

- *Multidisciplinarity*: Web applications can be characterized as a combination of print publishing and software development, marketing and computing, and art and technology (Powell et al. 1998). Therefore, the development of Web applications should be perceived as a *multidisciplinary approach* requiring knowledge and expertise from different areas. In addition to IT experts responsible for the technical implementation of the system, hypertext experts and designers should be employed to design hypertext and presentation, while domain experts should be responsible for the content. There is therefore a larger variety of competence and knowledge in the development team than in traditional software development.

Which discipline will dominate depends on the type of Web application. While e-commerce applications are based more on traditional database and programming expertise, developing a virtual exhibition would put more emphasis on domain and design expertise.

- *Young average age*: Web application developers are on average significantly younger – and thus less experienced – than traditional software developers. They usually live up to the stereotype of the "technology freak" who does not care too much about old conventions and is very interested in new tools and technologies (McDonald and Well and 2001b).

- *Community development*: The development of open source software freely available on the Web and its integration in "real" applications is a very recent phenomenon. Developers use this software for their own developments, which they in turn make available for the open source community. The conscious inclusion of external developers or groups of developers with their unwritten laws of cooperation is an important feature of this new form of community development.

Technical Infrastructure

The *inhomogeneity* and *immaturity* of the used components are important characteristics of the technical infrastructure of Web applications.

- *Inhomogeneity*: The development of Web applications depends on two external components: server and browser. While the Web server can usually be configured and operated as desired by the application programmers, there is no way to influence the users' Web browsers and their individual preferences. This situation is additionally complicated by different browser versions and their inter-operation with plug-ins (see section 1.3.2, Technical Context).

- *Immaturity*: Because of the increasing time-to-market pressure, components used in Web applications are often immature, i.e. they either have bugs or lack the desired functionality. Additionally, a version update of the Web application often entails a change of the development environment. As a result, development knowledge is often lost or cannot even evolve in the first place.

Process

The development process is the framework for all development-related characteristics, and is in turn influenced by *flexibility* and *parallelism*.

- *Flexibility*: In Web application development it is impossible to adhere to a rigid, predefined project plan. It is vital to react flexibly to changing conditions.
- *Parallelism*: Due to the necessity for short development times and the fact that Web applications can often be split up into autonomous components (e.g. authentication, search function, news ticker, etc.), many Web applications are developed in parallel by various subgroups of the development team. Contrary to traditional software development these subgroups are therefore structured according to these components and not according to the expertise of the project members (e.g. GUI developers, data modelers, etc.) (McDonald and Well and 2001b).

In addition to this *parallel development of application parts*, methodical tasks such as design, implementation and quality assurance are often carried out simultaneously for different versions. For example, quality assurance might be in process for an earlier version, while implementation has already begun for the next version and the following version is already being designed. This *parallel running of phases* poses new requirements for the planning of deployment of developers in Web projects.

Integration

A special characteristic of many Web applications is the need for *internal* and *external integration*. Integration in this context refers not only to technical aspects, but also to content, and organizational aspects.

- *Internal integration*: Frequently, Web applications have to be integrated with existing legacy systems when existing content, e.g. product catalogues, are to be made available through a Web application.
- *External integration*: In addition to internal integration, the integration of content and services of external Web applications is a special characteristic of Web applications. Despite strong similarities to heterogeneous database systems there are a number of particularities in integration on the Web (Lowe and Hall 1999, Sattler et al. 2002). First of all, there are a very large number of sources, frequently changing and with a high degree of autonomy concerning availability and schema evolution. Additionally, usually only few details are known about the properties of these sources, e.g. their content or functionalities. And finally, the different sources are often very heterogeneous at various levels, be it at the data level, the schema level, or the data model level.

The integration of external services, e.g. in portal-oriented Web applications, is based on the increasingly common development form of providing and using Web services (Weerawarana et al. 2005). A Web service in this context is a reusable component with an unambiguously defined interface and functionality. The interaction of different Web services, avoiding undesired side effects, and guaranteeing quality of service are but a few of the many relevant issues in this context.

1.3.4. Evolution

As mentioned above, evolution is a characteristic that governs all three dimensions of product, usage and development. The need for evolution can be argued for with the *continuous change* of requirements and conditions, the *competitive pressure*, and the general *fast pace* of development.

- *Continuous change*: Web applications change rapidly and are therefore subject to permanent evolution due to constantly changing requirements or conditions (Scharl 2000). The rapid and never-ending change of Web technologies and standards in particular makes it necessary to continuously adapt Web applications to these. This has two reasons: users want the newest Web hype, and the used tools are also technology-driven. This constant change of requirements and conditions is a central characteristic of Web applications. Changes may concern all three dimensions of a Web application – the product itself, its usage, and, in particular, its development.

- *Competitive pressure*: The extremely high competitive pressure on the Web, the time-to-market pressure and the necessity for a Web presence (comparable to the gold rush of the late 1840s (Murugesan 2000), increase the need for ever *shorter product lifecycles* and extremely *short development cycles* and apparently leave no room for a systematic development process. Immediate Web presence is considered more important than long-term perspective (Pressman 1998).

- *Fast pace*: The extreme time pressure on Web application development is due to the rapid change on the Web and the accordingly short life spans of Web applications or their frequency of updates. Tsichritzis sums it up very aptly in (Tsichritzis 2000): "either you are fast or irrelevant".

While for conventional software, evolution takes place in a planned series of versions, it is continuous for Web applications. This means that Web applications are in permanent maintenance. The cycle of change is often no longer than a few days or weeks (Pressman 2005). Web applications therefore require "lean" versions of traditional Software Engineering processes with special emphasis on requirements analysis and specification on the one hand and operation and maintenance on the other.

CHAPTER II

REQUIREMENTS ENGINEERING FOR WEB APPLICATIONS

Requirements Engineering (RE) covers activities that are critical for the success of Web engineering. Incomplete, ambiguous, or incorrect requirements can lead to severe difficulties in development, or even cause the cancellation of projects. RE deals with the principles, methods, and tools for eliciting, describing, validating, and managing requirements. In Web engineering RE has to address special challenges such as unavailable stakeholders, volatile requirements and constraints, unpredictable operational environments, inexperience with Web technologies, the particular importance of quality aspects such as usability, or performance. Therefore, when adopting existing RE methods in Web engineering, several important principles should be kept in mind: the involvement of important stakeholders; the iterative identification of requirements; awareness of the system architecture when defining requirements; and consequent risk orientation.

2.1. Introduction

Requirements play a key role in the development of Web applications. However, requirements are often not described properly and may be specified in an ambiguous, vague, or incorrect manner. Typical consequences of poor requirements are low user acceptance, planning failures, or inadequate software architectures.

RE deals with the principles, methods, and tools to identify, describe, validate, and manage requirements in system development. Today, numerous RE methods and tools are available. However, these approaches are often not applied by practitioners and RE is often performed in an ad-hoc manner, particularly in Web engineering. Although the complexity of today's Web applications require a more systematic approach, the maturity of the RE process is often insufficient.

Defining requirements is definitely not a new problem. In 1976 in their article entitled *Software Requirements: Are They Really a Problem?*, Bell and Thayer emphasize that requirements don't turn out automatically, but have to be identified in an engineering activity (Bell and Thayer 1976). In the early 1980s, Boehm studied the cost of defects in requirements and found that late removal of undiscovered defects is up to 200 times more costly than early identification and correction (Boehm 1981). In his article *No Silver Bullet: Essence and Accidents of Software Engineering*, Brooks stresses that the iterative collection and refinement of requirements are the most important functions of a software engineer for a customer (Brooks 1987).

There is a wide consensus about the importance of requirements for successful system development and over the years numerous standards, approaches, models, description languages, and tools have emerged. Nevertheless, the software industry is still struggling with massive difficulties when it comes to requirements:

- In a study conducted among 340 companies in Austria in 1995, more than two thirds of these companies regarded the development of a requirement document as a major problem in their development process. In addition, more than half of the companies perceived requirements management as a major problem (European Software Institute 1995).

- A survey among more than 8000 projects conducted by the Standish Group showed that 30% of all projects failed before completion and 70% of the remaining projects did not meet the expectations of customers. In more than half of the cases, the observed problems were closely related to requirements, including poor user participation, incomplete or volatile requirements, unrealistic expectations, unclear objectives, and unrealistic schedules (The Standish Group 1994).

- According to a study on the development of Web applications conducted by the Cutter Consortium only 16% of the systems fully meet the requirements of the contractors, while 53% of the deployed systems do not satisfy the required capabilities (Cutter Consortium 2000).

While there is general consensus on the importance and value of RE to meet schedule, budget, and quality objectives, there are often problems in the concrete adaptation and use of available processes, elicitation methods, notations, and tools. This is particularly true for the development of Web applications as there is still little experience compared with other domains and requirements are thus often acquired, documented, and managed in a very unsystematic way.

2.2. Fundamentals

2.2.1. Where Do Requirements Come From?

The individual objectives and expectations of stakeholders are the starting point of the requirement elicitation process. Stakeholders are people or organizations that have direct or indirect influence on the requirements in system development (Kotonya and Sommerville 1998). Important stake-holders are customers, users, and developers. Typical stakeholders for

Web applications include content authors, domain experts, usability experts, or marketing professionals. The objectives and expectations of stakeholders are often quite diverse, as demonstrated by a few examples:

- The Web application shall be available online by September 1, 2006 (*customer constraint*).
- The Web application shall support a minimum of 2500 concurrent users (*quality objective of customer*).
- J2EE shall be used as development platform (*technology expectation of developer*).
- All customer data shall be securely submitted (*quality objective of user*).
- The user interface shall support layouts for different customer groups (*quality goal of customer*).
- An arbitrary user shall be able to find a desired product in less than three minutes (*usability objective of customer*).
- A user shall be able to select an icon to display articles included in the shopping cart at any given time (*capability objective of user*).

The identification and involvement of success-critical stakeholders are central tasks of project management. A big challenge is to understand and reconcile the often conflicting objectives, expectations, backgrounds, and agendas. For example, there might be conflicts between a desired set of capabilities and the available budget; between the set of capabilities, the project schedule, and the desired quality; or perhaps between a desired development technology and the developers' skills and experiences. Understanding and resolving such contradictions and conflicts early on is crucial and an important contribution to risk management. Negotiation techniques have been proposed to support this task (Grunbacher¨ and Seyff 2005). In this process developing a shared vision among stakeholders is a pre-requisite for success.

Stakeholder objectives are often represented informally and provide the foundation for deriving more detailed requirements.

A *requirement* describes a property to be met or a service to be provided by a system. IEEE 610.12 defines a requirement as (1) a condition or capability needed by a user to solve a problem or achieve an objective; (2) a condition or capability that must be met or possessed by a system or system component to satisfy a contract, standard, specification, or other formally imposed documents; (3) a documented representation of a condition or capability as in (1) or (2).

Requirements are typically categorized as functional requirements, non-functional requirements, and constraints (Robertson and Robertson 1999). Functional requirements define a system's capabilities and services, while non-functional requirements describe desired levels of quality ("How secure?", "How usable?", etc.). Equally important, constraints are non-negotiable conditions affecting a project. Examples of constraints are the skill-level of the development team, the available budget, the delivery date, or the existing computer infrastructure in the deployment environment.

A *requirements document* summarizes all requirements and constraints agreed between the contractor and the customer (see also "Notations" in section 2.5).

It has been shown that the assumption of the waterfall model, i.e., defining complete, consistent, and correct requirements early on, is unrealistic in most projects (and in particular for Web application development). RE methods are thus often used in the context of iterative and agile life approaches. Current RE approaches therefore emphasize the identification and involvement of stakeholders, the negotiation and scenario-based discovery of requirements, an analysis of the organizational and social contexts prior to detailed modeling, and the clear definition of constraints affecting development (Boehm 2000b, Nuseibeh and Easterbrook 2000).

2.2.2. Requirements Engineering Activities

RE covers the elicitation, documentation, verification and validation, as well as the management of requirements throughout the development process.

Requirements Elicitation and Negotiation

Researchers have shown that "requirements are not out there to be collected by asking the right questions" (Nuseibeh and Easterbrook 2000). Rather, requirements are a result of a learning and consensus-building process (Boehm et al. 2001, Lowe and Eklund 2002). In this process, communication among the stakeholders is essential, as only their shared expertise can lead to mutually acceptable solutions. A wide set of methods and collaborative tools are available to facilitate communication and knowledge exchange in RE. Examples include creativity techniques, scenario-based methods, multicriteria decision processes, facilitation techniques, interviews, or document analysis (Nuseibeh and Easterbrook 2000).

Requirements Documentation

If stakeholders attain consensus, their agreements have to be refined and described in a *requirements document* in the degree of detail and formality that is appropriate for a project context. The choice of the appropriate degree of detail and formality (see section 2.5.2) depends on both the identified project risks and the experience and skills of the expected readers. Informal descriptions such as user stories, and semi-formal descriptions such as use cases, are particularly relevant in Web engineering.

Requirements Verification and Validation

Requirements need to be validated ("Did we specify the right things?") and verified ("Did we specify things correctly?"). There are several conventional methods for this purpose, such as reviews, inspections, or prototyping (Halling et al. 2003). In Web engineering, the openness of the Internet facilitates novel forms of direct user participation in requirements validation, e.g., through the online collection of user feedback (Deshpande et al. 2002).

Requirements Management

Rather than being stable, requirements are subject to frequent changes. Continuous changes of requirements and constraints are a major characteristic of Web projects. Methods and tools for requirements management support both the integration of new requirements and changes to existing requirements. They also help in evaluating the impact of changes by managing interdependencies among requirements, and between requirements and other development artifacts (*traceability*). Due to the difficulties of requirements management for even moderately complex systems, tools are typically used to support this task.

2.3.   RE Specifics in Web Engineering

How does RE for Web engineering differ from RE for conventional software systems? On the surface, the differences seem to be negligible as argued by researchers in the field: "While there are many differences between Web development and software development [. . .] there are also similarities between them. These include [. . .] requirements elicitation [. . .]" (Deshpande et al. 2002). However, if we take a closer look at some specifics, differences become apparent. The following subsections explore these by using the characteristics of Web applications discussed in Chapter 1 (Lowe 2003).

Multidisciplinarity

The development of Web applications requires the participation of experts from different disciplines. Examples include multimedia experts, content authors, software architects, usability experts, database specialists, or domain experts. The heterogeneity and multidisciplinarity of stakeholders make it challenging to achieve consensus when defining requirements. This problem is compounded as the people from different disciplines have their own languages and jargons that need to be reconciled.

Unavailability of Stakeholders

Many stakeholders, such as potential Web users, are still unknown during RE activities. Project management needs to find suitable representatives that can provide realistic requirements. For example, there is often a wide spectrum of possible users in Web projects and finding a reasonable set of representatives is hard.

Volatility of Requirements and Constraints

Requirements and constraints such as properties of deployment platforms or communication protocols are often easier to define for conventional software systems than for Web applications. Web applications and their environments are highly dynamic and requirements and constraints are typically harder to stabilize. Frequent examples of changes are technology innovations such as the introduction of new development platforms and standards, or new devices for end users.

Unpredictable Operational Environment

The operational environment of a Web application is also highly dynamic and hard to predict. Developers find it hard or impossible to control important factors that are decisive for the user-perceived quality of a Web application. For example, changing bandwidths affect the response time of mobile applications but are outside the sphere of the development team (Finkelstein and Savigni 2001).

Impact of Legacy Systems

The development of Web applications is characterized by the integration of existing software components such as commercial off-the-shelf products or open source software. In particular, Web developers frequently face the challenge to integrate legacy systems, for example when making existing IT systems of a company accessible through the Web. Developers are often asked to use existing components for economic reasons. The components that need to be integrated strongly influence the requirements and architectural style of the future system. Under such circumstances a waterfall approach to derive the system architecture from requirements will not succeed, as existing components, services, and the infrastructure define the range of possibilities and limitations for the developers. This means that, when identifying and defining requirements, Web developers have to be aware of the system architecture and architectural constraints. An iterative approach as proposed in the Twin Peaks model (see Figure 2-1) is more appropriate in such a context.

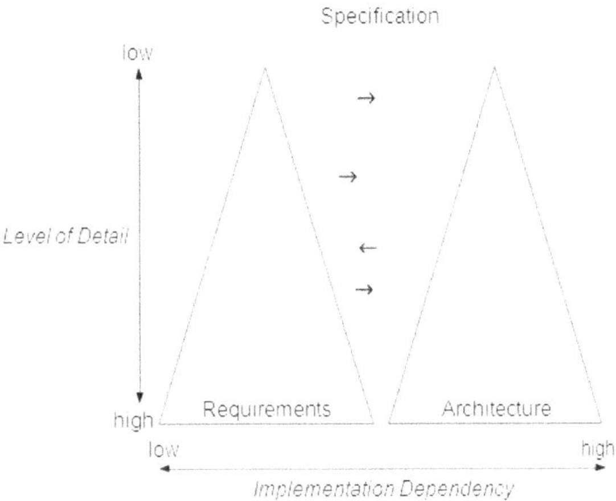

Figure 2.1: The Twin-Peaks Model (Nuseibeh 2001)

Significance of Quality Aspects

Quality aspects are decisive for the success of Web applications (Grunbacher¨ et al. 2004). Examples include the performance of a Web application, security as in e-commerce,availability, or usability. Despite the significance of quality aspects, developers have to deal with the problem that an exact specification of quality requirements is often hard or even futile before the actual system is built. For example, the response time of a Web application depends on many factors that are outside the control of the development team. A feasible approach for defining quality requirements is to specifying criteria for the acceptance test indicating whether or not a requirement has been met (see also an example of an acceptance criterion for a quality requirement in Table 2-1).

Quality of the User Interface

The quality of the user interface is another success-critical aspect of Web applications. When developing Web applications developers need to be aware of the IKIWISI (I Know It When I See It) phenomenon: users will not be able to understand and evaluate a Web application by just looking at abstract models and specifications; rather they need to experiment with it. It is thus absolutely essential to complement the definition and description of requirements by adding prototypes of important application scenarios (Constantine and Lockwood 2001).

Table 2.1: Formatted Specification

Attribute	Comment	Example
Id	Unique identifier	1.2.5
Type	Element from the requirement taxonomy	Learnability
Description	Short explanation in natural language	Web application X should be usable by occasional Web users without additional training.
Rationale	Explaining why the requirement is important.	Marketing managers are frequent users of the system.
Acceptance criterion	A measurable condition, which has to be met upon acceptance.	90% of the members of a randomly selected test group of occasional Web users can use the Use Cases 2.3, 2.6, 2.9, and2.11 without prior training.
Priority	An expression of the importance and the feasibility of the requirement.	Very important; hard to implement
Dependent requirements	List of requirements that depend on this requirement.	1.2.7, 2.3.4, 2.3.6.
Conflicting requirements	List of requirements that are in conflict with this particular requirement.	4.5.6
Further information	References to further information.	Usability Guidelines v1.2
Version history	A number of the revision to document the development history.	1.06

Quality of Content

Many traditional RE methods neglect Web content, though it is an extremely important aspect of Web applications.

In addition to software technology issues, developers have to consider the content, particularly its creation and maintenance. In the context of RE, it is particularly critical to define the required quality of content.

Important quality characteristics include accuracy, objectivity, credibility, relevance, actuality, completeness, or clarity (Strong et al. 1997).

Content management systems (CMS) gain importance and allow representing content concisely and consistently by separating content from layout, and offering content editing tools.

Developer Inexperience

Many of the underlying technologies in Web applications are still fairly new. Inexperience with these technologies development tools, standards, languages, etc. can lead to wrong estimates when assessing the feasibility and cost of implementing requirements.

Firm Delivery Dates

Many Web projects are design-to-schedule projects, where all activities and decisions have to meet a fixed final project deadline. The negotiation and prioritization of requirements are particularly crucial under such circumstances (Boehm et al. 2001).

2.4.　Principles for RE of Web Applications

The previous section discussed characteristics of Web applications and RE specifics in Web engineering. We have shown that RE for Web applications has to deal with risks and uncertainties such as volatility of requirements and constraints, inexperience of developers, or the impact of legacy solutions. A risk-oriented approach is a good choice to deal with these challenges. In this section we describe basic RE principles for Web applications. We derive these principles from the invariants of the win-win spiral model (Boehm 1996, Boehm 2000a), a risk-oriented and iterative lifecycle model that places particular emphasis on the involvement of the stakeholders and the elicitation and reconciliation of requirements. The win-win spiral model has influenced many state-of-the-art process models, including IBM's Rational Unified Process (RUP).

Web developers should keep the following principles in mind when performing RE activities:

Understanding the System Context

Many Web applications are still developed as isolated technical solutions, without understanding their role and impact in a larger context. A Web application can however never be an end in itself; it has to support the customer's business goals. For a Web application to be successful, it is important to clarify the system context (e.g., by analyzing and describing existing business processes) and the rationale of the system to be developed ("What are we doing this for?"). Developers have to understand how the system is embedded in its environment. Business analyses can determine the value of a Web application in relation to the resources it uses value driven requirements (Boehm 2000b). Understanding the system context also helps in identifying success-critical stakeholders, familiarizing with the intended use, and analyzing the constraints (Biffl et al. 2005).

Involving the Stakeholders

Success-critical stakeholders or their suitable representatives are at the heart of RE (Ginige and Murugesan 2001b) and their active and direct cooperation in identifying and negotiating requirements is important in each project phase. Project managers should avoid situations where individual project participants gain at the expense of others. It has been shown that such win-lose situations often evolve into lose-lose situations, causing the entire development project to suffer or even fail (Boehm et al. 2001).

The objectives, expectations, and requirements of stakeholders have to be acquired and negotiated repeatedly to address the dynamically changing needs in projects. We have shown that the multidisciplinarity and unavailability of stakeholders are specifics of RE for Web engineering. These characteristics lead us to derive the following requirements for the Web application context: (1) identification of success-effective stakeholders or suitable representatives (in case of unavailability); (2) understanding of stakeholders' objectives and expectations; and (3) negotiation of different expectations, experiences, and knowledge (multidisciplinarity). RE methods and tools have to be consistent with these requirements (see also section 2.5.3) and should contribute to the effective exchange of knowledge between the project participants, support a team learning process, the development of a shared vision among stakeholders, and help to detect conflicting requirements early. People know more than they say, so techniques for eliciting hidden knowledge are of particular interest.

Iterative Definition of Requirements

We have already discussed that a waterfall approach to requirements definition typical-ly does not work in highly dynamic environments and requirements should be acquired iteratively in Web application development. Requirements have to be consistent with other important development results (architecture, user interface, content, test cases, etc.). At project inception, key requirements are typically defined on a higher level of abstraction. These preliminary requirements can be used to develop feasible architectures, key system usage scenarios, and initial project plans. As the project progresses, development results can be gradually refined in more concrete terms, while continually ensuring their consistency. An iterative approach is necessary, especially in an environment with volatile requirements and constraints, to be able to react flexibly as the project evolves. If firm deadlines are mandated on the development team, then an iterative development approach allows selecting high-value requirements that need to be implemented first.

Focusing on the System Architecture

Existing technologies and legacy solutions have a high impact on the requirements of Web applications. The "solution space" thus largely defines the "problem space" and understanding the technical solution elements with their possibilities and limitations is essential. Requirements elicitation can never succeed in isolation from the architecture. This should be particularly taken into account when defining requirements. A consequent consideration of the system architecture allows developers to better understand the impact of existing solutions on these requirements and assess their feasibility. The Twin-Peaks model (Figure 2-1) (Nuseibeh 2001) suggests to concurrently refine both requirements and the system architecture in an iterative manner with a continually increasing level of detail.

Risk Orientation

Undetected problems, unsolved issues, and conflicts among requirements represent major project risks. Typical risk items are the integration of existing components into the Web application, the prediction of system quality aspects, or the inexperience of developers. A risk assessment should therefore been conducted for all requirements. The identified risks should be dealt with accordingly during the course of a project to make sure that risky system alternatives are not pursued. Risk mitigation has to take place as early as possible. This can include, for example, prototyping, to avoid the IKIWISI problem, early releases of a Web application to collect user feedback, or early incorporation of external components to avoid late and severe integration problems.

2.5.   Adapting RE Methods to Web Application Development

Today numerous methods, guidelines, notations, checklists, and tools are available for all activities in RE. However, in order to succeed developers should avoid a "one-size-fits-all" approach, and RE methods consequently have to be adapted to the specifics of Web engineering (see section 2.3) and the situation of specific projects. The principles described in section 2.4 guide the definition of a project-specific RE approach for Web engineering. Among others, developers have to clarify the following aspects during the adaptation process:

- Which types of requirements are important for the Web application? (section 2.5.1)
- How shall requirements for the Web application be described and documented? What are useful degrees of detail and formality? (section 2.5.2)
- Shall the use of tools be considered? Which tools are suited for the particular project needs? (Section 2.5.3).

2.5.1. Requirement Types

Both standardization bodies and commercial organizations have been developing a large number of taxonomies for defining and classifying various types of requirements. Examples are Volere (Robertson and Robertson 1999) or IEEE 830-1998. Most taxonomies distinguish between *functional* requirements and *non-functional* requirements. Functional requirements describe a system's capabilities and services (e.g., "The user can select an icon to view articles in the shopping cart at any given time."). Non-functional requirements describe the properties of capabilities and the desired level of services (e.g., "The Web application shall support at least 2500 concurrent users."). Other non-functional requirements refer to project constraints and system interfaces. In the following we briefly discuss types of requirements particularly relevant in Web development projects:

Functional Requirements

Functional requirements specify the capabilities and services a system is supposed to offer (e.g., money transfer in an online banking application). Functional requirements are frequently described using use case scenarios and formatted specifications (Cockburn 2001, Robertson and Robertson 1999, Hitz and Kappel 2005).

Contents Requirements

Contents requirements specify the contents a Web application should represent. Contents can be described, for example, in the form of a glossary.

Quality Requirements

Quality requirements describe the level of quality of services and capabilities and specify important system properties such as security, performance, or usability (Chung et al. 2000). The international ISO/IEC standard 9126 defines a technology-independent model for software quality which defines six quality characteristics, each divided into a specific set of sub characteristics. These six quality characteristics are:

- *Functionality* describes the presence of functions which meet defined properties. The sub characteristics are suitability, accurateness, interoperability, compliance, and security.
- *Reliability* describes a software product's ability to maintain its performance level under specific conditions over a defined period of time. The sub characteristics are maturity, fault tolerance, and recoverability.
- *Usability* describes the effort required to use a software product, and its individual evaluation by a defined or assumed group of users. The sub characteristics are understand-ability, learnability, and operability.
- *Efficiency* describes the ratio between the performance level of a software product and the resources it uses under specific conditions. Sub characteristics include time behavior and resource behavior.

- *Maintainability* describes the effort required to implement pre-determined changes in a software product. Its sub characteristics include analyzability, changeability, stability, and testability.
- *Portability* describes the suitability of a software product to be moved from one environment to another. The sub characteristics include adaptability, installability, conformance, and replaceability.

Initial attempts have been made by researchers to extend this basic model to Web-specific characteristics (Olsina et al. 2002).

System Environment Requirements

These requirements describe how a Web application is embedded in the target environment, and how it interacts with external components, including, for example, legacy systems, commercial-off-the-shelf components, or special hardware. For example, if a Web application is supposed to be ubiquitously available, then environment requirements have to specify the details.

User Interface Requirements

As Web users are expected to use a Web application without formal training, self-explanatory and intuitive guidance of users is critical for its acceptance. Requirements concerning the user interface define how a Web application interacts with different types of user classes. Important aspects are hypertext (navigation structure) and presentation (user interface). While navigation and presentation details are normally defined in the modeling process, initial decisions about the user interface strategy should be defined during requirements elicitation. Proto-types are best suited to avoid the IKIWISI problem. Constantine and Lockwood suggest that users should cooperate in the design of scenarios for specific tasks. Their *usage-centered design* approach is based on creating and iteratively fine-tuning models for roles, tasks, and interactions (Constantine and Lockwood 2002, Constantine and Lockwood 2001).

Evolution Requirements

Software products in general and Web applications in particular are subject to ongoing evolution and enhancement. Therefore, Web developers need to capture requirements that go beyond the planned short-term usage of an application. For example, a quality requirement demanding an additional 5000 concurrent users in two years has to be considered by defining a scalable system architecture. Evolution requirements are possible for all the types of requirements discussed so far, for example, future capabilities, future security requirements, etc.

Project Constraints

Project constraints are not negotiable for the project's stakeholders and typically include budget and schedule, technical limitations, standards, mandated development technology, deployment rules, maintenance aspects, operational constraints, legal, or cultural aspects affecting a project.

2.5.2. Notations

A large variety of notations are available for specifying requirements in different degrees of detail and formality. Examples include stories, formatted specifications, or formal specifications. The identified project risks provide guidance in choosing a suitable level of specification quality, i.e., to define how much RE is enough in a given project ("If it's risky to specify: don't–if it's risky not to specify: do"). In general, informal and semi-formal approaches are particularly suited for Web applications. (Kitapci et al. 2003) and Table 2-2 show different notations for requirements.

Stories

Stories are colloquial descriptions of desired properties; they are used to produce a common understanding between customers and developers. Examples are the user stories known from Extreme Programming (Beck 2000). A user story is formulated by a customer in her language and terminology, and describes problems and things the system should solve for that customer.

Table 2.2: Comparing the Suitability of Different Notations and Terminology, and Describes Problems and things the System should Solve for that Customer

	Precision	Ease of Validation	Effort	Non-Expert Suitability	Scalability
Stories			****	****	**
Itemized Requirements		*	***	****	***
Formatted Specifications	**	***	**	***	***
Formal Specifications	****	****			

A user checks the products she put in the online shopping cart. The input is validated as soon as the user clicks <Continue>. If no error is found, then the order will be accepted and a confirmation e-mail will be sent to the user.

Figure 2.2: Example of an Extreme Programming User Story

Figure 2-2 describes a short scenario from the customer's perspective:

Itemized Requirements

Itemized requirements are simple specifications in natural language. Each requirement has a unique identifier. One good example is a *data item description* as specified in IEEE/EIA-J-STD-016.

Formatted Specifications

Formatted specifications use an accurately defined syntax, but allow natural-language descriptions within this frame. Examples include use case descriptions in Unified Modeling Language (UML) (Cockburn 2001), the RDD-100 Requirements Specification Language, the MBASE SSRD Guidelines (Kitapci et al. 2003), or the Volere Shell (Robertson and Robertson 1999).

Table 2-1 shows an example of a formatted specification similar to the one suggested in (Kitapci et al. 2003). Important attributes are: *description, priority, rationale*, and *version history*. Each requirement is identified individually and can be referenced during the process at any given time using a unique id. Interdependencies with other requirements and other development results, such as architecture documents or plans, are captured to support traceability.

UML use cases are particularly useful to describe functional requirements. A *use case* describes a system's function from the perspectives of its actors and leads to a perceivable result for the actors.

An *actor* is an entity external to the system that interacts with the system. A *use case diagram* represents the relations between use cases and actors.

Use case diagrams are useful to depict high-level dependencies between use cases and actors. Use case details are defined in formatted specifications.

The attributes typically cover the number and name of the use case, the involved actors, pre- and post-conditions, progress description, exceptions and error situations, variations, source, rationale, trace links, or interdependencies with other UML diagrams.

Formal Specifications

Formal specifications are written in a language that uses a formally defined syntax and semantics. The most prominent example is "Z" (ISO/IEC13,568:2002). Formal specifications are hardly used for specifying Web applications, except in niche areas.

Suitability

Table 2-2 (Kitapci et al. 2003) compares the different notations with regard to the attributes accuracy, easy of validation, cost-effectiveness, suitability for non-experts, and scalability. A low to medium accuracy will be sufficient for specifying Web application requirements and a formal validation is normally not required. It is typically essential to keep the effort for eliciting and managing requirements low, and requirements should be understandable for non-experts. Finally, scalability is an issue due to the high complexity of many Web applications. We can see in Table 2-2 that informal and semi-formal description forms, e.g., stories, requirement lists, and formatted specifications, are particularly suited for Web applications.

2.5.3. Tools

We describe various classes of tools using the basic RE activities described in section 2.2.2. Existing RE tools are not limited to Web applications, but can be adapted to the specifics of Web application development.

Requirements Elicitation

In section 2.3 we mentioned that special emphasis should be placed on requirements negotiation in Web engineering. Negotiation methods and tools have been developed and explored in many disciplines as described in (Grunbacher¨ and Seyff 2005). *EasyWinWin* (Briggs and Grunbacher¨ 2002, Boehm et al. 2001, Grunbacher¨ and Braunsberger 2003) is a groupware-supported approach that guides a team of stakeholders in their efforts to jointly acquire and negotiate requirements. EasyWinWin defines a set of activities of a negotiation process.

A moderator guides stakeholders through the process. The approach uses group facilitation techniques that are supported by collaborative tools (electronic brainstorming, categorizing, polling, etc.). These activities are: review and expand negotiation topics; brainstorm stakeholder interests; converge on win conditions; capture a common glossary of terms; prioritize win conditions; reveal issues and constraints; identify issues, options; and negotiate agreements.

Requirements Validation

Due to the openness of the Internet, online feedback systems can complement or even replace more costly methods, such as personal meetings or interviews, when validating Web application requirements. For example, Internet users can be invited to participate in Web surveys to communicate their satisfaction with a Web application. Notice in this context, however, that due to the spontaneity of the interaction behavior, one can often observe neither approval nor denial, but simply indifference (Holck and Clemmensen 2002). If a Web user likes a Web application she will use it, but the user will be reluctant to spend time and cost on feedback (e.g.,information on errors found) to contribute to its development and improvement.

Requirements Management

Requirement management tools allow managing all requirements collected in a project in a central repository. In contrast to a word processing system, a requirements management tool stores requirements in a database. Similarly to formatted specifications, relevant attributes are managed for each of these requirements (see Table 2-1). Requirement management systems are important for change management and traceability of requirements. A good overview of existing tools can be found at (http://www.paper-review.com/tools/rms/read.php).

CHAPTER III

WEB APPLICATION ARCHITECTURES

The quality of a Web application is considerably influenced by its underlying architecture. Incomplete or missed architectural aspects make it difficult to realize the quality requirements of Web applications, or even make it totally impossible to meet them. Poor performance, insufficient maintainability and expandability, and low availability of a Web application are often caused by an inappropriate architecture. In addition to technical constraints like available Web servers, application servers used, or the integration of legacy systems, the architectures of Web applications should also consider the organizational framework in which they are embedded, e.g., the architect's experience. The use of flexible multi-layer architectures, the consideration of multimedia contents, and the integration of existing data repositories and applications are challenges in the development of successful architectures for Web applications. In addition to general properties of architectures, this chapter discusses the influence of existing architectural knowledge in the form of patterns and frameworks on the quality of Web applications. Moreover, this chapter explains typical Web application architectures and the components required to build them.

3.1. Introduction

When developing Web applications, we have to consider a large number of requirements and constraints (see section 2.5.1), ranging from functional requirements such as online product orders, over quality requirements such as performance or availability, to the integration of existing software systems–so-called legacy systems, or existing data repositories that our Web application should read. Also, Web applications are normally not developed "from scratch" as far as the technical infrastructure is concerned. Instead, we often have to extend or adapt an existing infrastructure. Besides pure technical constraints, we can identify other criteria, such as the economic viability of a technical infrastructure. The architecture of a Web application should be designed in such a way that it can best meet these requirements.

3.2. Fundamentals

3.2.1. What is an Architecture?

There is no unique definition of the term "architecture". For example, you can find more than 20 variants of the term on the home page of the renowned Software Engineering Institute (SEI) at Carnegie-Mellon University (http://www.sei.cmu.edu). Instead of adding another variant, we try to describe the most important properties of software architectures (according to Starke 2002):

- *Architecture describes structure*: According to (Bass et al. 1998), the architecture of a software system consists of its structures, the decomposition into components, and their interfaces and relationships. It describes both the static and the dynamic aspects of that software system, so that it can be considered a building design and flow chart for a software product.

- *Architecture forms the transition from analysis to implementation*: When we create architecture we try to break the functional requirements and quality requirements down into software components and their relationships and interfaces in an iterative approach. This process is supported by a number of approaches, such as the Unified Process.

- *Architecture can be looked at from different viewpoints*: Depending on the point of view from which architecture is seen, we can emphasize and itemize different architectural aspects. We normally distinguish between four different views (see also Kruchten 1995, Hofmeister et al. 1995): (1) the conceptual view, which identifies entities of the application domain and their relationships; (2) the runtime view, which describes the components at system runtime, e.g., servers, or communication connections; (3) the process view, which maps processes at system runtime, while looking at aspects like synchronization and con-currency; and (4) the implementation view, which describes the system's software artifacts, e.g., subsystems, components, or source code. This differentiation into different viewpoints is also supported by modeling languages, e.g., the *Unified Modeling Language – UML* (see, for example Booch et al. 1999).

- *Architecture makes a system understandable*: Structuring software systems and breaking them down into different perspectives allows us to better manage the complexity of software systems, and the systems become easier to understand. In addition, the abstraction of system aspects facilitates the communication of important architectural issues.

- *Architecture represents the framework for a flexible system*: Tom DeMarco (see DeMarco 1995) refers to architecture as a "framework of change", i.e., the software architecture forms the framework in which a software system can evolve. If extensions of a system have not been accounted for in advance, then such an extension will at best be difficult to realize.

Considering the above properties of architectures, we can easily see that architectural decisions are of enormous importance for the development of Web applications.

3.2.2. Developing Architectures

The requirements of software and thus its architecture are subject to change. Technical and organizational constraints change during and after the development of an application. This may be due to unclear requirements at the beginning of the development process or a change of requirements after a system's completion (see also section 1.3.4). This is the reason why software systems are often referred to as "moving targets". Figure 3-1 shows the different factors and constraints influencing the development of an architecture according to (Jacobson et al. 1999).

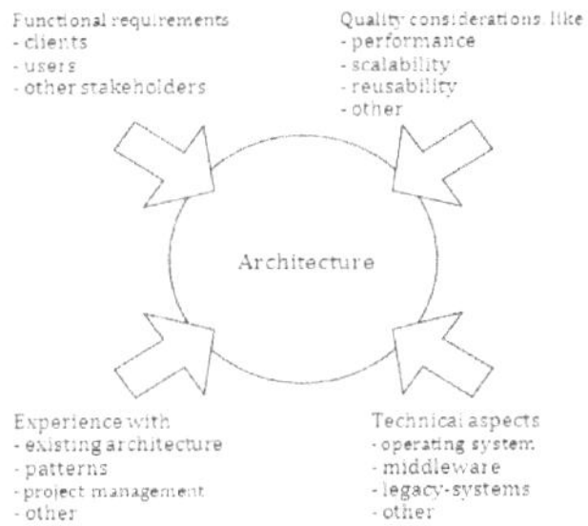

Figure 3.1: Factors Influencing the Development of an Architecture (according to Jacobson et al. 1999)

The architecture of an application is primarily influenced by functional requirements, i.e., the services provided by a system, and quality considerations such as scalability or performance. Apart from these requirements, architectures are further influenced by technical constraints, such as the used system software (e.g., the operating system), the middleware (e.g., a CORBA implementation), legacy systems to be integrated, standards used, development rules (e.g., coding guidelines), or distribution aspects (e.g., the distribution over different locations of a company). Moreover, the software architect's experiences play a considerable role in the definition of an architecture.

Because software systems are moving targets, architectures are typically developed in an iterative way. This approach should make the risks resulting from insecure requirements and constraints calculable and controllable. However, an iterative approach does not guarantee a good architecture. An iterative approach is not sufficient for solving specific design problems, such as the integration of a legacy system, in the development of an architecture. Fortunately, design patterns have proven to be very effective in supporting such design decisions.

Patterns

Patterns (see Gamma et al. 1997, Buschmann et al. 1996, Buschmann et al. 2000) describe recurring design problems, which arise in a specific design context, and propose solutions. A solution describes the participating components, their responsibilities, the relationship between these components, and the interplay of these components within the specific problem. This means that patterns enable us to reuse proven and consolidated design knowledge, supporting the development of high-quality software systems.

Buschmann et al. (1996) identifies patterns on three different abstraction levels:

- *Architecture patterns*: These patterns map fundamental structuring mechanisms for software systems. They describe architectural subsystems, their responsibilities, relationships, and interplay. One example of this type of pattern is the *Model-View-Controller* (*MVC*) pattern (Buschmann et al. 1996, p.125).

- *Design patterns*: These patterns describe the structure, the relationships, and the interplay between components to solve a design problem within a defined context. Design patterns abstract from a specific programming language, but they move within the scope of architecture patterns. An example of a design pattern is the *Publisher-Subscriber* pattern described in (Buschmann et al. 1996), p. 339.

- *Idioms*: describe patterns that refer to a specific implementation in a programming language, such as, for example, the *Counted-Pointer* idiom for storage management in C++ (Buschmann et al. 1996), p. 353.

Patterns are available for different infrastructures, e.g., for J2EE and CORBA (Malveau and Mowbray 1997).

Nevertheless, patterns can only represent a guideline for the problem at hand. The software architect has to adapt patterns to the respective problem and constraints. In addition, the architect need to integrate and tune the used patterns. To support the integration process, (Buschmann et al. 2000) recommends so-called pattern languages. A *pattern language* describes the interconnections of related patterns on different abstraction levels, suggests different uses for patterns, and shows the adaptation needed to ensure a sound system. Buschmann et al. (2000) introduces an example of a pattern language for distributed systems.

With their *patterns for e-business*, (IBM 2002) describes architecture patterns for commercial applications and how they can be mapped to the IBM infrastructure. These architecture patterns are refined along a decision chain, ranging from the use case to the target architecture.

Frameworks

Frameworks represent another option to reuse existing architectural knowledge. A framework is a reusable software system with general functionality already implemented. The framework can be specialized into a ready-to-use application (see also Fayad et al. 1999). The framework serves as a blueprint for the basic architecture and basic functionalities for a specific field of application. This means that the architectural knowledge contained in a framework can be fully adopted in the application.

However, the benefits of a framework, i.e., the simple reuse of architecture and functionality, have to be weighed against its drawbacks, i.e., a high degree of training effort, a lack of standards for the integration of different frameworks, and the resulting dependence on manufacturers.

3.2.3. *Categorizing Architectures*

A number of architectures for specific requirements in several application domains have been developed in the past few years. Anastopoulos and Romberg (2001) and Bongio et al. (2003) describe architectures for Web application environments, taking the layering aspect of architectures, or the support of different data and data formats – the data aspect of architectures – into account:

- *Layering aspect*: Layering means that software systems are structured in several tiers to implement the principle of "separation of concerns" within a software system. Many frameworks in the field of distributed systems and Web applications are primarily structured by the layering aspect, e.g., J2EE (Sun Microsystems 2003a) Architectures used to integrate legacy systems, also referred to as *Enterprise Application Integration (EAI)*, and portals also fall in this category.
- *Data aspect*: Data can be structured or non-structured. Structured data follow a defined scheme like tables in a relational database or XML structures in a document. Non-structured data are multimedia contents, e.g., images, audio, and video, which typically do not follow an explicit scheme. This makes their automatic processing difficult.

The increasing distribution of software systems has led to the development of architectures and infrastructures addressing the distribution of data and messages:

- *Distributed Object Middleware (DOM)*: This type of infrastructure allows to access remote objects transparently. It is based on the *Remote Procedure Call (RPC)* mechanism. Some DOM systems also enable objects on different platforms to interact (e.g., CORBA). Other examples of this type of system include Microsoft's DCOM (Distributed Component Object Model), or EJB (Enterprise Java Beans) by Sun Microsystems.

- *Virtual Shared Memory (VSM)*: The VSM model lets distributed processes access common data. The processes themselves access a shared memory. An appropriate middleware, transparent for the processes, is used to distribute the data. This data can be "any-where" in the system (hence "virtual"). Examples of VSM systems include Corso (http://www.tecco.at) and Equip (http://www.crg.cs.nott.ac.uk).

- *Message Oriented Middleware (MOM)*: MOM systems offer functionalities for asynchronous transmission of messages. Asynchronous communication differs from synchronous communication in that messages are sent to the receiver regardless of its status, e.g., the receiver may not be available when the message is sent, i.e., he or she may be offline. MOM ensures that messages are delivered nevertheless. Examples of MOM systems include Sun's JMS (Java Messaging Service) and Microsoft's MSMQ (Microsoft Message Queue).

- *Peer to Peer (P2P)*: P2P stands for direct communication between two devices – the *peers* – in a system without using a server, i.e., they communicate over a point-to-point connection. The peers are basically equal. P2P systems describe how the devices in such a network communicate and how they can "discover" each other. Examples of P2P systems include JXTA (http://www.jxta.org) and X middle (http://xmiddle. sourceforge.net/).

- *Service Oriented Middleware (SOM)*: SOM enhances DOM systems by the concept of services. A service in this context is a number of objects and their behavior. These objects use a defined interface to make a service available for other systems/services. SOM defines communication protocols between services, and provides for location-and migration-transparent access to services, thus supporting a simple integration of services beyond platform boundaries. One example of a SOM is Sun's Jini system (http://www.sun.com/software/jini/). Architectures emerging within the field of Web services also belong to this category.

These architectures are applicable to distributed systems in general, which means that they are not limited to Web applications. This is why we will not discuss these architectures in detail in this chapter.

3.3. Specifics of Web Application Architectures

Chapter 1 describes the characteristics of Web applications from the usage, product, development, and evolution perspectives. One remarkable development concerns quality requirements for Web applications. We can see that Web application requirements are more demanding than requirements for comparable traditional software systems. This development, especially with regard to changeability, performance, security, scalability, and availability, has encouraged the proposal and introduction of specific technical infrastructures both for the development and the operation of Web applications.

Thus, we have to distinguish web infrastructure architecture on the one hand and web application architecture on the other. Jablonski et al. (2004) refer to the former as Web Platform Architectures (WPA) and to the latter as Web Application Architectures (WAA). As WAA strongly depend on the problem domain a web application is in, this chapter will focus primarily on WPAs.

Web Platform Architectures have been developed for a wide variety of problems. Application servers, like implementations of the J2EE (Sun Microsystems 2003a) and .NET platform (Beer et al. 2003), try to provide basic services for session handling, protocol wrapping, and data access. Beside application servers, specific architectural solutions have been developed for issues like security, performance, or data integration. Examples of these are firewalls, caching proxies, and EAI respectively.

Paradoxically, the use of this wide range of different systems has made it increasingly difficult to evaluate and maintain distinct quality requirements. For example, meeting performance requirements becomes more and more difficult due to the increasing number of components and products used from third-party (commercial or open source) vendors.

Other problems in the development of Web applications are the in homogeneity and immaturity of technical infrastructures (see also section 1.3.3). Gorton and Liu (2002) describes problems in preparing performance analyses for application servers due to quickly evolving updates: The survey disclosed that newly introduced product versions have been slower than their predecessors, and that new functionalities have caused incompatibilities in the existing application code. Only after extensive adaptations, which required an extremely detailed knowledge of the products concerned, was it possible to restore the desired performance behavior.

Regardless of the in homogeneity and immaturity problems, current Web applications use a large number of different technical infrastructures to solve given problems. The range extends from technical open-source frameworks, such as Struts (http://jakarta.apache.org/struts/)

and Cocoon (http://xml.apache.org/cocoon/), over application servers like EJB implementations, to portal frameworks like Brazil (http://research.sun.com/brazil/) and JetSpeed (http://jakarta.apache.org/jetspeed/). In addition, many Web applications use several frameworks concurrently. Lanchorst et al. (2001) gives a categorization and analysis of different frameworks. Another aspect that becomes noticeable in the field of Web application architectures is the internationalization of Web applications, requiring the support of different languages, character sets, and representation mechanisms (e.g., representation of Arabic characters from right to left) on the WPA level. Many of these aspects are supported by programming languages, or operating systems. For example, the Java platform offers internationalization mechanisms, reaching from different character encodings (e.g., ISO-8859-1, UTF-8) to multi-language user interfaces by using so-called "resource bundles".

All these different aspects need to be considered when developing architectures for web applications. In particular WPAs provide a wide range of functionalities to solve common problems and they define the context in which web applications may evolve. The following section gives an overview of common components of Web platform architectures and shows how these architectures support the development of Web applications.

3.4. Components of a Generic Web Application Architecture

Figure 3-2 shows the basic components of Web architectures and their relationships. Communication between these components is generally based on the request – response principle, i.e., one component (e.g., a Web browser) sends a request to another component (e.g., a Web server), and the response to this request is sent back over the same communication channel (synchronous communication).

The following list briefly describes each of these components:

- *Client*: Generally a browser (*user agent*) is controlled by a user to operate the Web application. The client's functionality can be expanded by installing plug-ins and applets.
- *Firewall*: A piece of software regulating the communication between insecure networks (e.g., the Internet) and secure networks (e.g., corporate LANs). This communication is filtered by access rules.
- *Proxy*: A proxy is typically used to temporarily store Web pages in a cache. Howev-er, proxies can also assume other functionalities, e.g., adapting the contents for users (customization), or user tracking.

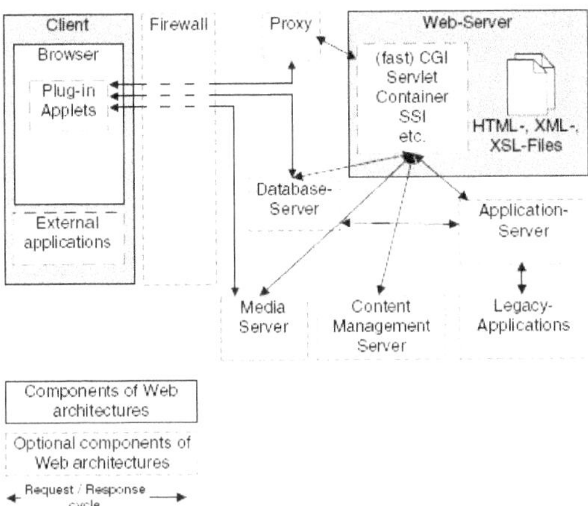

Figure 3.2: Basic components of Web Application Architectures

- *Web server*: A Web server is a piece of software that supports various Web protocols like HTTP, and HTTPS, etc., to process client requests.

- *Database server*: This server normally supplies an organization's production data in structured form, e.g., in tables.

- *Media server*: This component is primarily used for content streaming of non-structured bulk data (e.g., audio or video).

- *Content management server*: Similar to a database server, a content management server holds contents to serve an application. These contents are normally available in the form of semi-structured data, e.g., XML documents.

- *Application server*: An application server holds the functionality required by several applications, e.g., workflow or customization.

- *Legacy application*: A legacy application is an older system that should be integrated as an internal or external component.

3.5. Layered Architectures

3.5.1. 2-Layer Architectures

A 2-layer[1] architecture according to (Anastopoulos and Romberg 2001), also called *client/ server* architecture, uses a Web server to provide services to a client (see Figure 3-3).

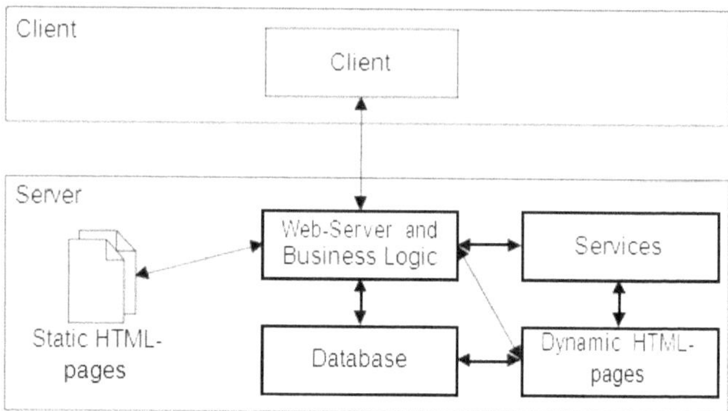

Figure 3.3: A 2-Layer Architecture for Web Applications (according to Anastopoulos and Romberg 2001, p. 40)

The 2-layer architecture can take different forms within the environment of Web applications. A client request can point directly to static HTML pages, without requiring any processing logic on the server layer, or it can access a database via the application logic on the Web server (e.g., in the form of CGI scripts). Dynamic HTML pages include script instructions directly in the HTML code, e.g., when SSI (Server-Side Include) is used, and they are interpreted either by databases with HTML functionalities or by a Web server. The application logic, or dynamic HTML pages, can use services (e.g., user identification or data encryption) when the HTML response is generated.

This architecture is suitable particularly for simple Web applications. In contrast, a multi-layer architectural approach is required for more demanding applications which are accessed by a large number of concurrent clients or which provide complex business processes requiring the access to legacy systems, amongst others.

3.5.2. N-Layer Architectures

N -layer architectures allow us to organize a Web application in an arbitrary number of layers (see Figure 3-4). They typically consist of three layers, the data layer, providing access to the application data, the business layer, hosting the business logic of the application in an application server, and finally the presentation layer, which renders the result of the request in the desired output format. Additionally, security mechanisms like firewalls, or caching mechanisms like proxies, can be integrated into the request-response flow upon demand. 2-layer and n-layer architectures differ mainly in how they embed services within the application server component. Services like customization or workflow are held in the application server's context, so that they are available to all Web applications. Wu and Zhao (2003) describe services and their interconnections with respect to workflow, security and business logic. Similarly, (Horvat et al. 2003) describe horizontal and vertical services, a terminology introduced with CORBA, in a portal architecture. Xiang and Madey (2004) describe a multi-layer service architecture using semantic Web services to support the development of Web applications.

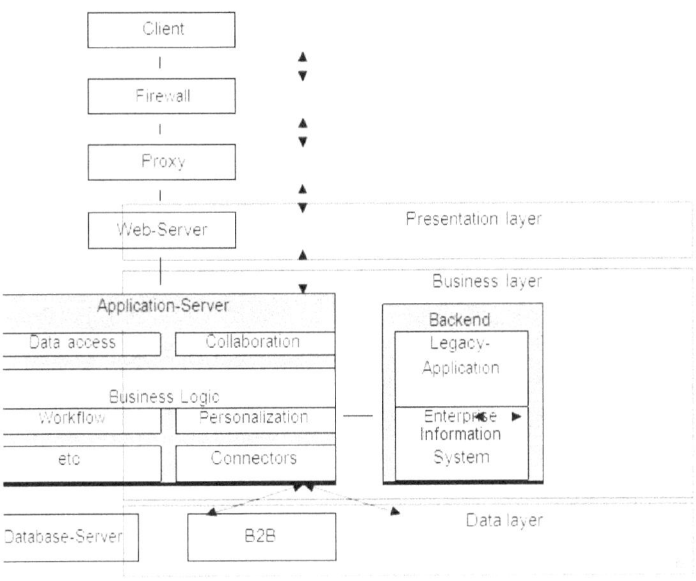

Figure 3.4: An n-Layer Architecture for Web Applications (According to Anastopoulos and Romberg 2001, p. 42).

Services are embedded in the application server with a defined interface, and the same interface can be used to manage these services. The WebSphere application server with its WebSphere Business Components is a good example of these functionalities. As a further advantage, Web applications profit from the distribution and load balancing mechanisms of the application server.

What's more, so-called *connectors* can be used to integrate external systems, e.g., business partner systems, or to integrate legacy applications and enterprise information systems.

Many commercial application servers have been optimized for the processing of database contents, while the support of multimedia contents and hypertext structures has been neglected. One example of a possible integration of video data into an application server is available at (http://www.ibm.com/software/data/informix/blades/video/). The WebRatio modeling tool can map hypertext aspects onto J2EE and .NET (Ceri et al. 2003). This means that expansions have been implemented on top of existing implementations, such as J2EE. We will have a closer look at some of these expansions and concepts in the following subsections.

JSP-Model-2

Sun Microsystems' JSP-Model-2 (Java Server Pages) architecture (http://java.sun.com/ developer/technicalArticles/javaserverpages/servlets jsp/) implements the MVC pattern for Web applications, thus laying the foundation for the integration of navigation aspects, internationalization, and multi-platform delivery in Web applications (see Figure 3-5).

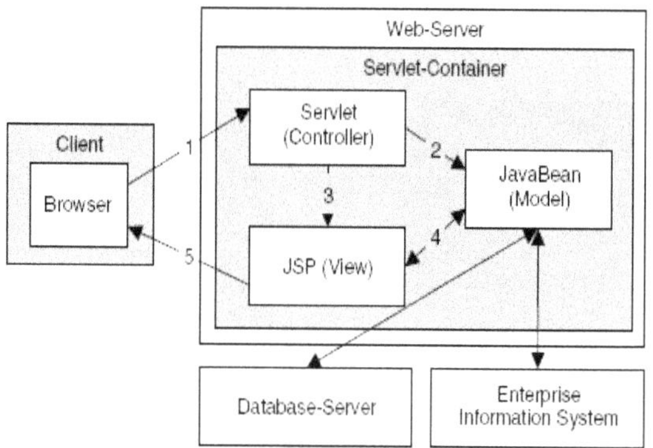

Figure 3.5: The JSP-Model-2 Architecture

The JSP-Model-2 architecture is deployed on a Web server, i.e., view, controller, and parts of the model functionalities of this pattern are available over a Web server extension – a *servlet container*. The controller, i.e., the flow and control logic of the Web application, is implemented in the form of servlets, which are software components running in a servlet container. The controller is responsible for providing access to the application logic (model) and selecting the graphical presentation (view). JavaBeans, i.e., software components representing the application's data, are used to implement the model. The model itself normally accesses backend systems, such as a database or legacy application. The graphical presentation is realized by Java Server Pages (JSP)

Struts

The JSP-Model-2 architecture is enhanced by the Struts open-source project of the Apache Software Foundation (http://struts.apache.org/). Struts offers useful additions for Web applications, such as error handling and internationalization. In addition, Struts uses an XML configuration file which allows the control of the processing flow within the MVC pattern to facilitate the processing of client requests.

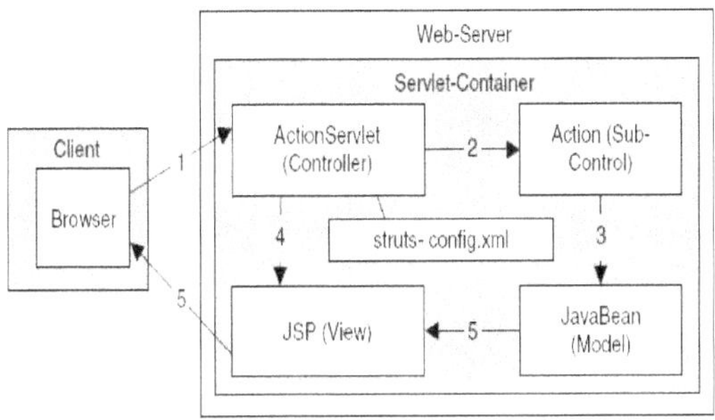

Figure 3.6: JSP-Model-2 Implementation in Struts

Figure 3-6 shows how the Struts framework processes a user request: Initially, each user request (1) is received by the central ActionServlet. This servlet reads the request's URI to find the controller (Action) the request is to be forwarded to (2), i.e., the application logic that should be executed for this request. The controller is responsible for selecting or creating a model in the form of a JavaBean, which can be represented in a view (3). Based on the selected model, and perhaps other information (user information, user agent, etc.), the ActionServlet can now select a view to represent the contents (4). Finally, the selected view generates the output, which is sent to the user (5). In contrast to the original JSP-Model-2, Struts allows to configure the view and model allocation in the (struts-config.xml) file. This means that the content can be presented more flexibly, either for reasons of adaptation, or for multi-platform deliveries.

Similar to the JSP-Model-2, Struts lets you implement various output formats computed by configured JSP pages. In its standard installation, the framework offers no way to use other visualization technologies, e.g., XSLT . However, there are various products that enhance Struts, trying to close this gap. For example, StrutsCX supports XSLT to generate different output formats (http://it.cappuccinonet.com/strutscx/index.php).

OOHDM-Java2

The OOHDM-Java2 approach specified in (Jacyntho et al. 2002) describes how the OOHDM navigation model is mapped onto the J2EE platform. Its implementation is based on the MVC pattern. Figure 3-7 shows how OOHDM-Java2 components are mapped to the MVC pattern. In contrast to JSP-Model-2 and Struts, this approach introduces an explicit navigation component. The WebRatio tool supports the modeling and coding of the different components.

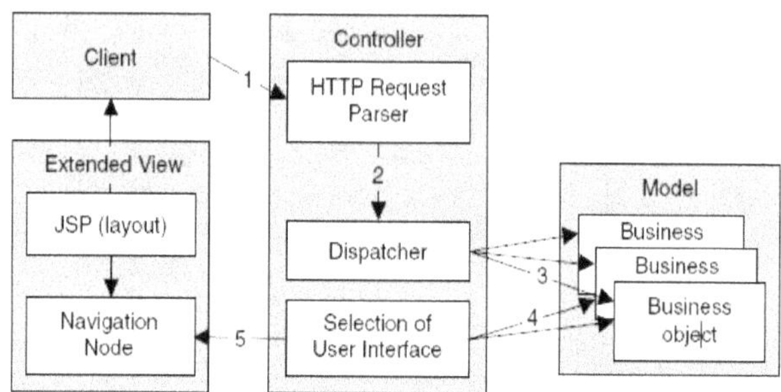

Figure 3. 7: OOHDM-Java2 Components (according to Jacyntho et al. 2002)

In this figure, the execution sequence is indicated by the numbered edges: (1) An HTTP request is issued to the HTTP Request Parser, which forwards a message to the Dispatcher (2). Similar to Struts, this parser runs the allocated application objects (3). Subsequently, the selected application object or other information (e.g., user agent) is used to identify the user interface (4). Next, the user interface is enriched by navigation aspects (5). And finally, the result is put in an appropriate layout and transmitted to the client.

Proxies

Proxies were originally used to save bandwidth, which is the reason why early proxies were referred to as *caching proxies* (Bongio et al. 2003), p. 353. But proxies are capable of assuming a number of other functionalities as well:

- *Link proxy*: Link proxies exist in at least two types. First, systems like Persistent URLs (PURLs, see Weibel et al. 1999) use proxy-like components. More specifically, a proxy is used as an intermediate server to forward client requests for URLs to the (actual) server. If the name or location of the requested resource changes, then its address (URL) only has to be changed internally, and the client doesn't have to know this. Such a change requires a mapping table between the requested URL and the "real" URL. This mapping table is maintained by the proxy. Second, proxies are used to adapt and format links and contents to users (e.g., Webcosm Hill et al. 1996). One of the ideas behind this concept is to dynamically insert links matching a user's interests. This means that the HTML pages are analyzed in the proxy and modified to match the user profile. The user will be informed about the fact that the transmitted resource was changed at the bottom of the document.

- *History proxy*: Many Web applications try to adapt their functionalities to users. However, this attempt is normally accompanied by the problem that HTTP is a stateless protocol, i.e., no information whatsoever about the history of a user navigation is available across several Web sites. For example, if a user plans a vacation trip and books a flight, a hotel, and a rental car on the Internet, then the airline ticket vendor does not typically know that the user also booked a hotel and a rental car. If the airline company knew this information, then both the hotel and the rental car could be canceled if the user cancels the flight. A similar problem arises in the field of direct marketing. The more details about a user's interests are known, the more consumer-oriented an advertising effort can be. Proxies can be used to manage a user's history. More specifically, the proxy assigns a unique ID for a user and stores this ID using cookie technology. Now, if the user visits the Web site of another company also connected to the same proxy, then this user information can be retrieved, enabling a unique user identification. This approach records and evaluates a user's behavior within such an information aggregate, i.e., all Web sites sharing the same proxy. The Boomerang server of DoubleClick (http://www.doubleclick.com) uses this concept for direct marketing. Of course, the use of such technologies is a critical point with regard to the privacy of users.

Integration Architectures

External or internal systems, e.g., existing applications, existing databases and interfaces to external business partners, can be integrated into Web applications on three levels: the presentation level, the application logic level, and the content level. Integration architectures address integration aspects on the content level and the application logic level and are commonly summarized under the term *Enterprise Application Integration* (*EAI*) architectures. This category also includes architectures which integrate existing applications as a whole, i.e. content as well as application logic is integrated. Strictly speaking, EAI focuses on the integration of legacy systems. Alternatives to EAI are Web services , which support the integration of services, i.e., application logics and contents. On the presentation level, a set of different systems is typically integrated by using portal architectures.

EAI has emerged from the field of business-to-business integration, requiring existing systems to be closely coupled, from purchasing over production planning to billing. This integration can be implemented in any of the following ways:

- *Point to point*: The applications exchange the content to be integrated via external communication mechanisms, e.g., file transfer or batch transactions.
- *Data delivery*: A system supports access to internal data directly, e.g., over a database access.
- *Data integration*: Several applications use the same data storage, e.g., via a jointly used database.
- *Delivery of functionalities*: A legacy system allows to access functionalities, e.g., over an API.
- *Reconstruction of functionalities*: Access to functionalities is transparent to the client, i.e., a functionality can, but does not have to, be implemented directly in the legacy system.
- *Porting*: Legacy systems are migrated onto Web platforms, replacing the original system.

Figure 3-8 shows an architecture used to integrate legacy systems which uses *wrappers* to integrate legacy systems. This integration approach uses specific middleware, which usually consists of application servers combined with XML technologies. One example of this approach is the J2EE-Connector architecture, which specifies the integration of legacy systems into a J2EE environment (Sun Microsystems 2003b)!

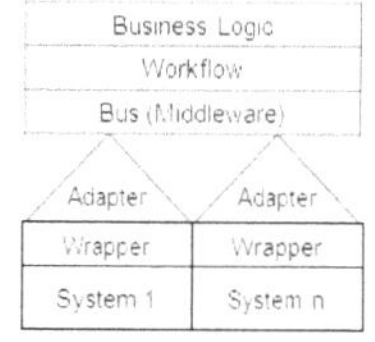

Figure 3.8: Example of an EAI Architecture

The major drawback of most current integration approaches is that the application logic and data in legacy systems can be accessed only in their entirety. This has a negative impact on the adaptability and reusability of both the data and the application logic. Another problem is due to the different development paradigms used by legacy systems and Web applications. For example, not all legacy systems support transaction mechanisms in the same way as relational database systems do.

These problems normally result in a situation where the integration of legacy systems becomes a costly and time-consuming venture, not least due to the fact that many legacy systems are poorly documented, and their developers are often no longer available. Portals represent the most recent development of multi-layered Web applications. Portals try to make contents, which are distributed over several nodes of different providers, available at one single node providing a consistent look and feel. Figure 3-9 shows a schematic view of the basic architecture of a portal server.

Portal servers are based on so-called *portlets*, which arrange contents and application logics in a navigation structure and layout appropriate for the portal. An independent aggregation component is used to integrate the set of different portlets into a uniform Web site. This aggregation can be specified by the portal provider, or manipulated by the user, e.g., through customization. One example of a portal server is the JetSpeed open-source project (http://portals.apache.org/).

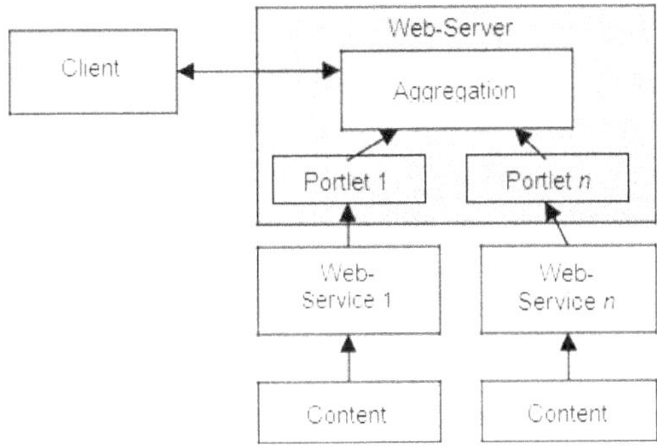

Figure 3.9: Example of a Portal-Oriented Web Application Architecture

A number of unsolved problems makes the integration of external Web applications more difficult, including the fact that both the performance and scalability of the final system cannot be predicted. This usually means that we can't predict the response time or the avail-ability of embedded components. Consequently, requirements with regard to the quality of service become an important issue when integrating external services, similarly to multi-media information. Examples for initiatives in this field include the *Web Service Endpoint Language* (http://www.w3.org/2001/04/wsws-proceedings/rod smith/text13.htm) and the *DAML Services Initiative* (www.daml.org/services/index.html).

3.6. Data-Aspect Architectures

Data can be grouped into either of three architectural categories:

1. Structured data of the kind held in databases.
2. Documents of the kind used in document management systems.
3. Multimedia data of the kind held in media servers. In this respect, Web applications are normally not limited to one of these data categories.

They rather integrate documents, media, and databases. We will have a closer look at these categories in the following sections.

3.6.1. Database-Centric Architectures

A number of tools and approaches is available to integrate databases into Web applications. These databases are accessed either directly from within Web server extensions (in the case of 2-layer architectures), or over application servers (in the case of *n*-layer architectures). Since database technologies (and particularly relational databases) are highly mature, they are easy to integrate. APIs are available for different platforms, e.g., *Java Database Connectivity (JDBC)* for Java-based applications, or *Open Database Connectivity (ODBC)* for Microsoft technologies (Saake and Sattler 2003), to access relational databases. Bongio et al. (2003) describes the design of data-intensive Web applications.

3.6.2. Architectures for Web Document Management

In addition to structured data held in databases and multimedia data held on media servers, contents of Web applications are often processed in the form of documents . Content management architectures support the integration of documents from different sources, representing a mechanism to integrate these contents into Web applications. This section discusses important aspects for architectures used to integrate external contents. A detailed description of the functionalities and tasks involved in content management systems, i.e., systems that implement content management architectures, is found in the literature, e.g., in (Jablonski and Meiler 2002).

Figure 3-10 shows the components of a content management architecture. A Web server receives a client request and forwards it to a *content delivery server*. The content delivery server is responsible for distributing – and perhaps caching – the contents. If a requested content is not in the cache, then the request is forwarded to the *content management server*.

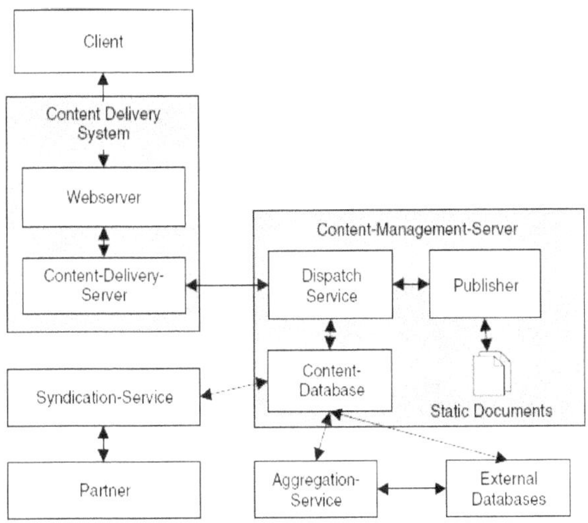

Figure 3.10: A content Management Architecture for Web Applications (according to Anastopoulos and Romberg 2001)

The content can be available directly on that server (in static form as a document, or in a content database), or it can be accessible externally. Depending on the type of integration, external content can be retrieved either by accessing external databases (directly or by use of an aggregation service), or from a syndication *service*. In contrast to accessing a database, syndication services can handle additional functionalities, e.g., automated billing of licensing rights.

One example of a publisher component to prepare static XML documents is the Cocoon 2 open-source framework. Cocoon 2 supports the publication of XML documents in the Web. Its range of application is primarily the transformation of XML contents documents into different output formats. The underlying processing work is based on a *pipeline model* (see Figure 3-11), i.e., a request is accepted and forwarded to a generator pre-defined in a configuration file. Within the pipeline, the XML document is subject to several processing steps to bring it into the desired output format. All processing steps in the pipeline can access information about the request, e.g., the user agent, to adapt the response to the request (e.g., customization of the user interface).

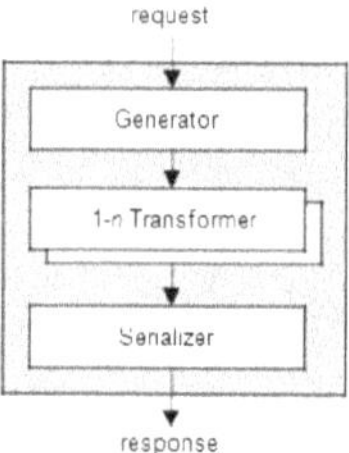

Figure 3.11: The Cocoon 2 Pipeline

The *generator* is called at the beginning of the process; it is responsible for parsing the XML document. The generator uses the SAX parser to read the XML document, and then generates SAX messages, called *events*. The generator has to forward these events to the pipeline. These SAX events can be used to transform or forward the document. This means that the generator makes data available for processing.

The *transformer* can be compared with an XSL stylesheet. Finally, a *serializer* is responsible for converting to the desired output format, e.g., HTML or XML again. A powerful configuration mechanism in the form of an XML configuration file can be used to select and define generator, transformer, and serializer. For example, the configuration routine lets one control the processing pipeline, depending on the request and the processing results.

3.6.3. *Architectures for Multimedia Data*

The ability to handle large data volumes plays a decisive role when designing systems that use multimedia contents. While the data volume is normally not decisive in database-centric Web applications, it influences the architecture and the design of multimedia Web applications considerably. A detailed overview of architectural issues concerning multimedia data in Web applications can also be found in (Srinivasan et al. 2001).

Basically, multimedia data, i.e., audio and video, can be transmitted over standard Internet protocols like HTTP or FTP, just like any other data used in Web applications. This approach is used by a large number of current Web applications, because it has the major benefit that no additional components are needed on the server. Its downside, however, is often felt by users in that the media downloads are very slow. We can use *streaming* technologies to minimize these waiting times for multimedia contents to play out. Streaming in this context means that a client can begin playout of the audio and/or video a few seconds after it begins receiving the file from a server. This technique avoids having to download the entire file (incurring a potentially long delay) before beginning playout. The contents have to be transmitted in real time, which requires a corresponding bandwidth, and low jitter, to ensure continuous playout of the contents. A guaranteed transmission bandwidth is appropriately called *quality of service* (see also section 1.3.2).

Two protocols are generally used for the streaming of multimedia contents. One protocol handles the transmission of multimedia data on the network level, and the other protocol controls the presentation flow (e.g., starting and stopping a video) and the transmission of meta-data. One good example of a network protocol is the *Real Time Protocol* (*RTP*), which collaborates with a control protocol, the *Real Time Streaming Protocol* (*RTSP*). In addition to these popular protocols, there are several proprietary products, e.g., *Progressive Networks Audio* (*PNA*) and *Progressive Networks Metafile* (*PNM*) of RealNetworks (http://www.real. com), or the *Microsoft Media Server* (*MMS*) protocol.

We can identify two distinct fields of application for multimedia data streaming. First, making existing contents available on demand, e.g., video-on-demand, and second, broadcasting live contents to a large number of users, e.g., Web casting. Each of these two use cases poses totally different requirements on the network, and the hardware and software architectures. While each user establishes his or her own connection to the server in an on-demand scenario (see Figure 3-12), causing major bandwidth and server load problems, broadcasting makes especially high demands on the network level. Examples are given in (Srinivasan et al. 2001) and (Roy et al. 2003). Ideally, a server used for broadcasting should manage one single media stream, which is simultaneously broadcasted to all users by the network infrastructure (e.g., by *routers*), as visualized in Figure 3-13. However, since multicasting is not supported generally in the Internet, the server has to use point-to-point connections, similar to the on-demand scenario, to "simulate" the broadcast functionality.

In order to keep such systems scalable to the desired number of users, it is often necessary to distribute multimedia data (e.g., on caching proxies) to keep the users' access paths as short as possible. This approach forwards a user's request to the nearest node that holds the required data. The distribution itself can be based on either a push or a pull mechanism. The *push* mechanism won't transmit the contents to a local node unless at least one user or a specific number of users requested them. This mechanism is typically used when there is no information about the spatial distribution of the user group. In contrast, the *pull* mechanism transmits the contents by a pre-defined distribution plan, which means that the media distribution can be optimized with regard to the transmission medium (e.g., satellite) and the transmission time (e.g., over night). Of course, this type of distribution needs to know the local distribution of the user group. Building such a distribution infrastructure is very costly and maintenance-intensive, which is the reason why it is not widely used.

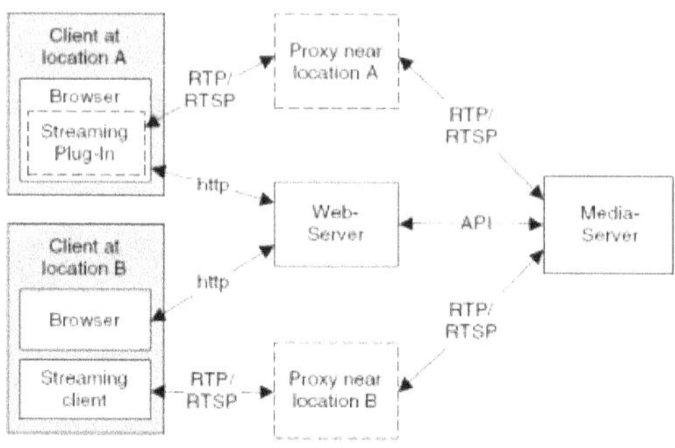

Figure 3.12: Streaming Media Architecture using Point-to-Point Connections

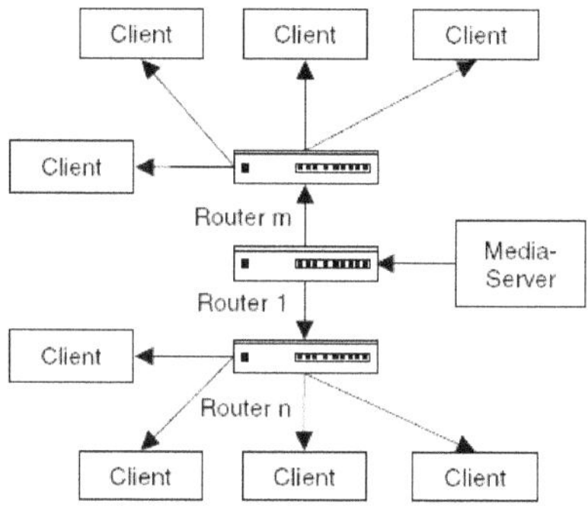

Figure 3.13: Streaming Media Architecture using a Broadcasting Infrastructure

Another unsolved problem is the poor interactivity of media, since special browser plug-ins (e.g., Apple's QuickTime Player, or Microsoft's Windows Media Player) are normally used to visualize multimedia contents, but these plug-ins have no way of representing links or anchors. An additional problem occurs for time-sensitive media, such as audio and video, because the contents of an HTML page – text and images – cannot be synchronized to a medium's contents. However, languages like SMIL (Synchronized Multimedia Integration Language) try to overcome this limitation and thus can be used to specify media interaction features.

CHAPTER IV

MODELING WEB APPLICATIONS

It is not (yet) common to model Web applications in practice. This is unfortunate as a model-based approach provides a better alternative to the *ad-hoc* development of Web applications and its inherent problems. As mentioned in previous chapters, these are for example insufficient fulfillment of requirements, faulty specification, or missing system documentation. Models represent a solid starting point for the implementation of a Web application taking into account static and dynamic aspects of the content, hypertext, and presentation levels of a Web application. While the content model of a Web application which aims at capturing underlying information and application logic is similar to the corresponding model of a non-Web application, the need to consider the hypertext is particular to Web applications. The hypertext model represents all kinds of navigation possibilities based on the content. The presentation model maps hypertext structures to pages and their links thus represent the graphical user interface.

The inclusion of context information, such as user, time, location, and device used, and the adaptation of the Web application which is "derived" from this information, has gained increasing attention in modeling efforts.

This is undoubtedly a consequence of ubiquitous Web applications that have become increasingly popular. This chapter discusses the spectrum of existing methods and some tools available to model Web applications and their highlights to help the reader select a suitable modeling method. Such methods are the basis for model-based development and code-generation tools, which allow us to consider the use of different Web clients and run-time platforms.

4.1. Introduction

To build a dog house you simply need two skillful hands, the required materials, and a few tools to quickly start hammering and sawing and achieve an attractive result, depending on your personal creativity.

Nobody, however (Booch et al. 1999), would set about building a skyscraper with the same naïve light-heartedness – the result would surely be fatal! What's clear to everybody when it comes to building a skyscraper is often ignored when it comes to building complex Web applications. A systematic approach and a specification of the Web application to be built in the form of visual models are recommended if we need to develop complex Web applications.

4.2. Fundamentals

Engineering disciplines have successfully used models to reduce complexity, document design decisions, and facilitate communication within project teams. Modeling is aimed at providing a specification of a system to be built in a degree of detail sufficient for that system's implementation. The result of a modeling process are models representing the relevant aspects of the system in a simplified and – ideally – comprehensible manner.

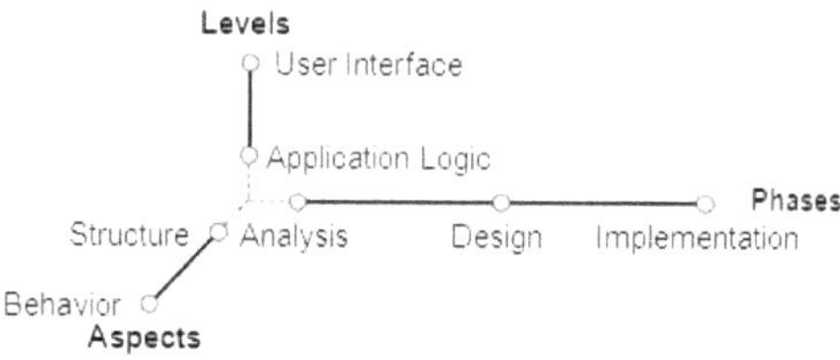

Figure 4.1: Requirements of Software Application Modeling.

Computer science has also been using the modeling approach to develop software for some time. In this field, the object of modeling is the application to be created. Figure 4-1 shows that the scope of modeling spans along three orthogonal dimensions. The first dimension traditionally comprises the application logic level and the user interface level in the sense of an encapsulation of the "what" and "how" of an application. Aspects known as structure (i.e., objects, their attributes, and their relationships to other objects) and behavior (i.e., functions and processes), both of the application logic and the user interface, form another dimension. Since an application cannot be developed "in one shot", but has to be gradually refined and expanded during the development process, the development phases form the third application modeling dimension. Through successive refinements the requirements identified in the requirements analysis are transformed to analysis models first and design models later, on which the implementation will be based. The roots of modeling are found on the one hand in Data Engineering and, on the other hand, in Software Engineering. Historically, Data Engineering modeling focuses on the structural aspects, i.e., the data aspects of an application. Identification of entities, their grouping and their relation-ships is the major focus. The best-known model in this respect is the *Entity-Relationship* (*ER*) model (Chen 1976). In contrast, modeling in Software Engineering focuses on behavioral aspects, to fulfill the needs of programming languages. Today, it is mainly based on an object-oriented approach. The most important characteristics of object-oriented modeling are a holistic approach to system modeling and the central concept of the object, comprising structure and behavior.

The Unified Modeling Language (UML) (OMG 2004, Hitz et al. 2005) is an object-oriented modeling language and seen as a kind of *lingua franca* in object-oriented software development; it forms the basis of most modeling methods for Web applications. UML allows to specify the aspects of a software system in the form of models, and uses various diagrams to represent them graphically. UML has two types of diagrams: structural diagrams such as class diagrams, component diagrams, composite structure diagrams, and deployment diagrams, as well as behavioral diagrams, such as use case diagrams, state machine diagrams, and activity diagrams.

4.3.   Modeling Specifics in Web Engineering

The tools of the trade in Web application modeling are basically not new, however, methods to model traditional applications are not expressive enough for specific characteristics of Web applications (see also section 1.3). For example, traditional modeling languages (such as UML) do not provide appropriate concepts for the specification of hyperlinks. This was the reason why special modeling approaches for Web applications have been developed during the past few years, which allow to address a Web application in the three dimensions introduced above, i.e., levels, aspects, and phases.

4.3.1.   Levels

To model Web applications, the document-like character of its content as well as its non-linear hypertext navigation has to be taken into account. This is the reason why we distinguish three levels when modeling Web applications, as shown in Figure 4-2, in contrast to the two levels used in the modeling methods for traditional applications. The three levels are *content*, i.e., the information and application logics underneath the Web application, *hypertext*, i.e., the structuring of the content into nodes and links between these nodes, and the *presentation*, i.e., the user interface or page layout. Most methods which are used to model Web applications follow this separation into three levels (Fraternali 1999).

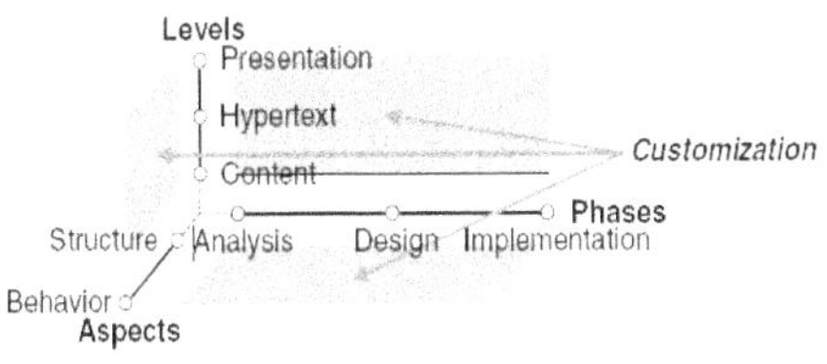

Figure 4.2: Requirements of Web Application Modeling

A clear separation of these three levels allows reuse and helps to reduce complexity. For example, we could specify a number of different hypertext structures that will do justice to the specific requirements of different user groups and used devices for a given content. The aim of a content model is the explicit definition of the information structure. Comparable to a database schema in data modeling this eliminates redundancies. This means that the structure of the information will remain unchanged, even if the information itself changes frequently.

To design efficient navigation, content may be offered redundantly on several nodes on the hypertext level. Due to the separation of concerns, content is just modeled once in the content model and the hypertext structure model just references the corresponding content. In this way, users can find this information over several access paths. To prevent users from getting lost while navigating and to keep the cognitive stress on users as low as possible, hypertext modeling should rely on recurring navigation patterns (Bernstein 1998).

In turn, when modeling the presentation level, the focus is on a uniform presentation structure for the pages to achieve a brand recognition effect for the Web application among its users. Although the visual appearance of a Web application is of importance, aesthetic aspects are not within the major focus of modeling.

Despite a separation of concerns and the different objectives at the three levels, we would like to map the levels to one another. To achieve this mapping between levels, level inter-dependencies have to be captured explicitly.

For example, different personalized hypertext access paths could be mapped onto one single content model. A comprehensive model of a Web application includes all three levels discussed here, however, the emphasis can vary depending on the type of Web application. Web applications that provide a purely hypertext-oriented user interface to a large data set will probably require the modeling focus to be on content and hypertext structure. In contrast, presentation-oriented Web applications, e.g., corporate portals or online shopping malls, will most likely have larger demands on presentation modeling.

4.3.2. Aspects

Following the object-oriented principles, structure and behavior are modeled at each of the three levels, i.e. at content, hypertext and presentation. The relevance of the structure and behavior models depends on the type of Web application to be implemented. Web applications which make mainly static information available require less behavior modeling compared with highly interactive.

Web applications, such as for example e-commerce applications which provide search engines, purchase order functions, etc. With respect to mapping the different levels, it is recommended to use a uniform modeling formalism for structure and behavior, which might allow relying on one single CASE tool. Naturally, this modeling formalism has to cope with the specific characteristics of each of the three levels.

4.3.3. Phases

There is no consensus in literature about a general modeling approach for the development of Web applications. In any case, the sequence of steps to model the levels should be decided by the modeler.

Depending on the type of Web application, it should be possible to pursue an information-driven approach, i.e., starting with content modeling, or a presentation-driven approach, i.e., starting with modeling of the application's presentation aspects. Model-based development in Web engineering contradicts somewhat the often found practices in Web projects comprising, e.g., short-lived development cycles and the desire for "agile methods" (see section 10.5).

A model-based approach counters this situation with a comprehensive specification of a solution model and, if appropriate case tool support is available, the possibility to automatically generate the (prototypical) Web application.

Models also ensure the sustainability of solution ideas, in contrast to shorter-lived software solutions. In addition, the communication amongst the developers of a team as well as between customers and developers is improved.

4.3.4. Customization

The inclusion of context information in the development of Web applications plays a significant role to allow for e.g. personalization, multi-delivery and location-based services. Customization considers the context, e.g., users' preferences, device characteristics, or bandwidth restrictions, and allows to adapt the Web application accordingly. It influences all three Web modeling dimensions of content, hypertext, and presentation with respect to structure and behavior and should be taken into account in all phases of the development process. Handling context information is, therefore, treated as an independent modeling dimension.

Since there is currently no wide-spread modeling method that covers all dimensions discussed here , we will use UML as our notation in this chapter and expand it by borrowing a few concepts from a UML-based Web application modeling method, namely *UWE (UML-based*

Web Engineering) (Koch and Kraus 2002). We suggest using UWE as UWE is compliant with UML. It is defined as a UML profile that is a lightweight extension of UML.

4.4.   Modeling Requirements

As shown in Chapter 2 various techniques can be used to identify, analyze, describe, evaluate, and manage Web application requirements. Use cases are the preferred modeling technique for functional requirements, not least since they can be represented graphically. The overall functionality of a Web application is modeled as a set of use cases, which describe the Web application requirements from the actors' (people and other systems) perspectives. Additionally, use cases can be supplemented by UML activity diagrams to describe the functional requirements in more detail.

One peculiarity of Web application requirements is navigation functionality, which allows the user to navigate through the hypertext and to find nodes. (Baresi et al. 2001) suggests separating the functional from the navigational use cases, creating two distinct models. Another approach (UWE), selected herein, is to create one single use case model, which uses the UML navigation stereotype to denote the difference between functional and hypertext-specific use cases.

All Web applications have at least one human user, most often anonymous. In our example of an online conference paper reviewing system (referred to as "the reviewing system" in the following), four actors can be identified: users of the reviewing system, authors submitting papers to the conference, members of the program committee (reviewers) reviewing papers submitted, and the chair of the program committee (PC chair).

Figure 4-3 shows a use case diagram representing part of the use case model for the reviewing system, which will serve as the starting point for further modeling. Navigational requirements supplementing functional requirements are made explicit through the stereotype navigation in the use case diagram.

Use cases should be described in detail. We can describe each use case in textual form or by use of a behavior diagram, e.g. an activity diagram.

Activity diagrams are mainly used when use cases are based on more complex application logic. Such a use case, for example, might be implemented as a Web service. Figure 4-4 is an example of a simplified paper submission process.

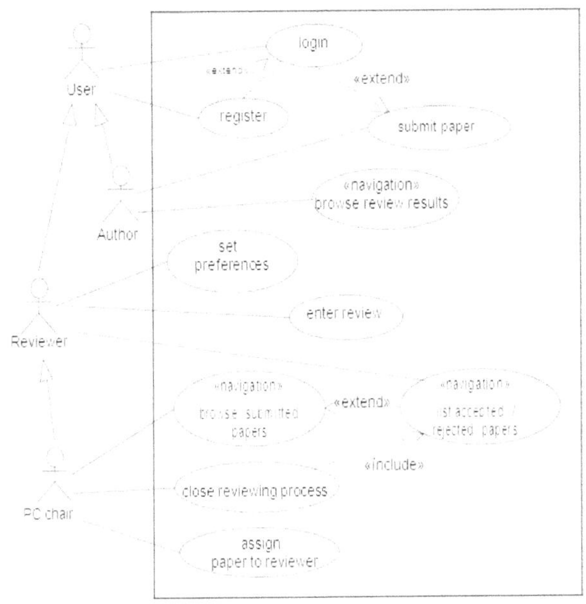

Figure 4.3: Use Case Diagram of the Reviewing System

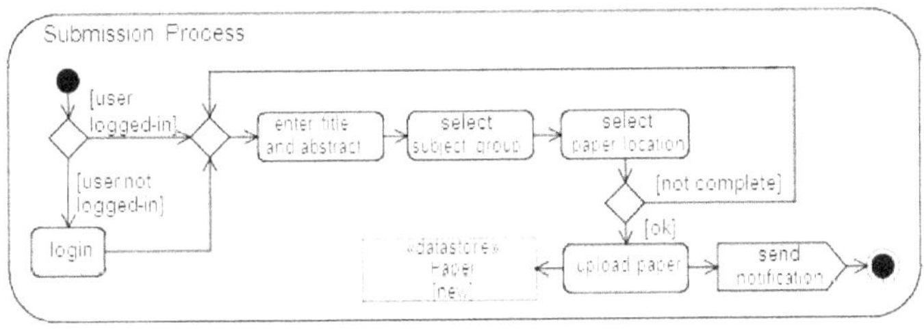

Figure 4.4: Activity Diagram of the Submission Process

4.5. Content Modeling

The information provided by a Web application is one of the most important factors for the success of that application, not least due to the origins of the Web as an information medium . Modeling the content in the sense of pure data modeling is normally sufficient for static Web applications. Complex Web applications (according to the categorization defined in Chapter 1) additionally require the modeling of behavioral aspects. This means that content modeling includes the creation of the problem domain model, consisting of static and dynamic aspects, as known from traditional Software Engineering. In addition the following Web application characteristics have to be taken into account:

- *Document-centric character and multimedia*: It is necessary to take all kinds of different media formats into account when modeling the content, including the structures the information is based on.
- *Integration of existing data and software*: Many Web applications build on existing data repositories and software components, which were not created for Web applications originally. Content modeling has to satisfy two potentially contradicting objectives, i.e., it should cover the content requirements of the Web application to the best possible extent, and it should include existing data structures and software components.

4.5.1. Objectives

Content modeling is aimed at transferring the information and functional requirements determined by requirements engineering to a model. The hypertext character of a Web application and the requirements of its presentation will not be considered in this effort.

Content modeling produces a model that comprises both the structural aspects of the content, e.g., in the form of a class diagram, and, depending on the type of Web application, the behavioral aspects, e.g., in the form of state and interaction diagrams.

4.5.2. Concepts

As mentioned earlier, content modeling builds on the concepts and methods of data modeling or object-oriented modeling. It strives to ensure that existing information is free from redundancies and reusable.

Figure 4-5 shows a very simplified UML class diagram for the reviewing system example. The diagram models a conference to be held on a number of topics, and users who can sign in to the conference and submit their papers. A paper is subject to a review by three reviewers. Notice the invariant attached to the class "Paper": it ensures that authors won't be able to review their own papers. This class diagram will later serve as the basis to model the hypertext and the presentation for the example application.

In addition to the class diagram, Figure 3-6 shows a state machine diagram used to model the various states of a paper in the reviewing system. It shows that a submitted paper will be assigned to three reviewers for review after the submission deadline has expired. If a pre-set threshold value is reached, the paper is accepted; otherwise, it is rejected. In both cases the authors are notified via email about the outcome of the review. Finally, an accepted paper will be printed once the final version has been submitted.

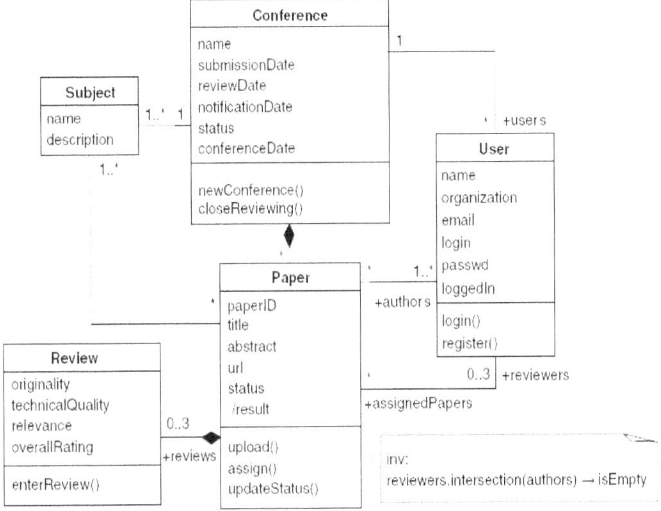

Figure 4.5: Class Diagram for the Reviewing System

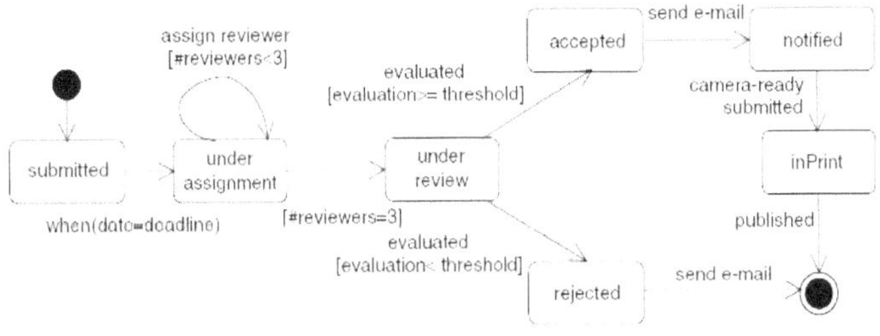

Figure 4.6: State Machine Diagram for the States of a Paper

4.6. Hypertext Modeling

The non-linearity of hypertext is one of the most important properties to be taken into account when modeling Web applications. Thus the hypertext structure has to be designed carefully. This can be achieved by using suitable access structures, i.e., navigation options, to avoid the risk of users getting lost and putting them under excessive cognitive stress.

4.6.1. Objectives

The objective of hypertext modeling – also known as navigation modeling – is to specify the navigability through the content of a Web application, i.e., the navigation paths available to the users. Hypertext modeling generates a two-fold result: First, it produces the *hypertext structure model*, also known as navigation *structure model* which defines the structure of the hypertext, i.e., which classes of the content model can be visited by navigation. Second, it refines the hypertext structure model by access elements in the form of an *access model*.

Hypertext modeling focuses on the structural aspects of the hypertext and the access elements. The navigational behavior of a Web application is normally not represented explicitly, because it provides very little additional information for the developer.

4.6.2. Hypertext Structure Modeling Concepts

In contrast to the content level, for which ER diagrams or class diagrams are used, specialized notations are often employed to model the hypertext structure. Hypertext structure modeling is based on the concepts of hypertext, i.e., on nodes (also called pages or documents) and links between these nodes.

The starting point used for the creation of a hypertext structure model is usually the content model which contains the classes and objects to be made available as nodes in the hypertext. Often the hypertext structure model is specified as a view on the content model and is therefore some-times also called the navigational view. Thereby a node is specified as a view on the content model selecting one or more objects from the content. Some methods even define transformation rules to derive links on the basis of relationships on the content level. Additional links can be added by explicit design decision. Other methods model the hypertext structure independently of the con-tent model. For example the OOHDM (Object-Oriented Hypermedia Design Method) (Schwabe et al. 2002) offers an approach to model scenarios, where the hypertext structure model can be built directly from the navigational requirements identified by these scenarios.

In any case, we can create various hypertext structure models that define hypertext views on the content. For example, if we take into account the access rights of different users for the hypertext structure modeling, we can obtain personalized hypertext views.

In the reviewing system example hypertext views are required for the following user roles: author, reviewer, and PC chair. Figure 4-7 shows the hypertext structure model for the PC chair's view. A PC chair can view all submitted papers. In addition, the PC chair can access the list of accepted or rejected papers, and the reviewer profiles. In line with the UWE modeling method, Figure 4-7 shows how the UML stereotype navigation class is used to mark classes representing nodes in the hypertext structure model to distinguish them from content classes. Links are modeled by directed associations with the stereotype navigation link.

The literature defines various specific types of links to further refine the semantics of the hypertext structure model. For example, the HDM (Hypertext Design Model) method (Garzotto et al. 1995) specifies the following types of links:

- *Structural links* connect elements of the same node, e.g., from a review summary to the review details.
- *Perspective links* put various views of a node in relation to each other, e.g., the PostScript and the PDF versions of a paper.

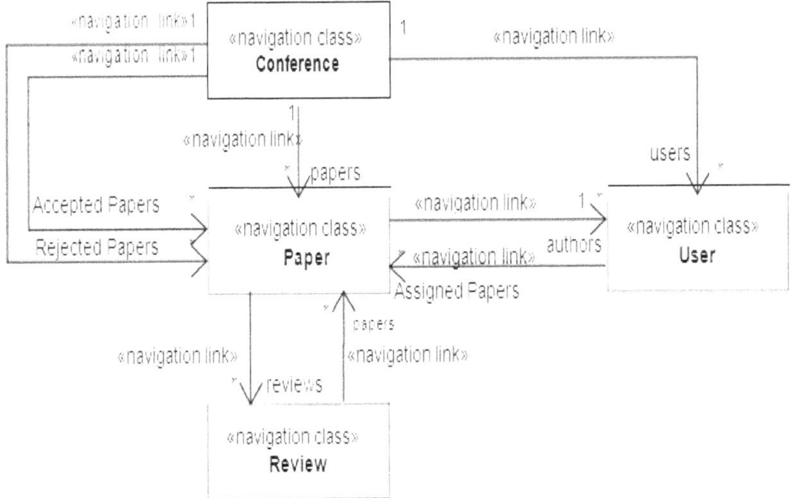

Figure 4.7: Hypertext Structure Model of the PC's View on the Reviewing System

- *Application links* put different nodes in relation to each other, depending on the application, e.g., a link pointing to "best paper".

Other classifications are based on the possible transport of information during navigation. For example, the WebML (Web Modeling Language) method (Ceri et al. 2003) specifies the following types of links:

- *Contextual links* carry context information, e.g., the unique number of a reviewer, to navigate from one reviewer to the reviews he or she created.
- *Non-contextual links* have no associated context information, e.g., links pointing from a single review to the list of all reviews.

With regard to the distribution of nodes on the hypertext level over pages on the presentation level, WebML specifies additionally the following types of links:

- *Intra-page links* are used when the source and the destination of a link belong to the same page, e.g., when a link allows the user to directly navigate to the summary of a paper, which is displayed further down on the page.
- *Inter-page links* are used when the source and the destination are on different pages, e.g., when detailed information about the authors and their papers are on different pages.

Based on the functional requirements of Web applications, the UWE (Koch and Kraus 2002). modeling method defines the following types of links:

- *Navigation links* are used to navigate between nodes, e.g., links between papers and their authors.
- *Process links* point to the start node of a process, e.g., to the beginning of the review submission.
- *External links* point to a node not directly belonging to the application, e.g., to the formatting guidelines established by the publisher of the conference proceedings, which are not directly stored in the reviewing system.

The OO-H (Object-Oriented Hypermedia) modeling method (Gomez´ and Cachero 2003) defines five types of links as follows:

- *I-links (internal links)* point to nodes inside the boundaries of a given navigational requirement, e.g., internal links to review details of one of the reviewers.
- *T-links (traversal links)* point to nodes covering other navigational requirements, e.g. from an author to his or her papers.
- *R-links (requirement links)* point to a start of a navigational path, e.g., to add a new review.
- *X-links (external links)* point to external nodes, e.g., to external formatting guidelines.
- *S-links (service links)* point (with their corresponding response links) to services, e.g., to an external search engine.

4.6.3. *Access Modeling Concepts*

The hypertext structure model built so far alone is not sufficient to describe how nodes can be reached by navigation. To allow users to navigate to nodes the users need navigation and orientation aids. These are formulated in the form of *access structures* refining the hypertext structure model. Recurring access structures are described in (German and Cowan 2000, Lyardet et al. 1999, Rossi et al. 1998, Akanda and German 2005) as design patterns, also called "hypermedia design patterns" or "navigation patterns". The use of these navigation patterns helps to increase the quality of the hypertext model tremendously.

In our reviewing system example, if one wants to navigate from a reviewer to a paper assigned to this reviewer, one will have to identify this specific paper during navigation. For example, this could be realized in the form of a list showing all papers. Such a selection list for navigational support is also known as an "index". An *index* is an access structure which allows users to select a single object (i.e. one object of the content) out of a homogeneous list of objects. In contrast, a *menu* allows users to access heterogeneous nodes, or further menus (i.e. submenus). Other access structures are the guided tour and the query. A *guided tour* allows users to sequentially walk through a number of nodes. A *query* allows users to search for nodes. Most modeling methods offer dedicated model elements for the most frequently used navigation patterns. Special navigation patterns include *home*, which points to the home page of a Web application, and *landmark*, which points to a node that can be reached from within all nodes.

Some of these access structures can be added to the hypertext structure model automatically (Koch and Kraus 2002). For example, indexes can be added automatically whenever we want to allow access to a set (>1) of objects of a node.

Figure 4-8 shows a simplified access model of the PC chair's view specified in the hypertext structure model in our reviewing system. Note that a link's default multiplicity is 1.

The PC chair has access to all papers, reviews, and users. To access a specific paper, a unique number is used. Alternatively, the PC chair can search for a paper by title. UWE uses UML stereo-types, i.e., menu (e.g., "Conference"), index (e.g., "ReviewingStatus"), query(e.g., "SearchPaperByTitle"), and guided tour , to specify the menu, index, query, and guided tour access structures.

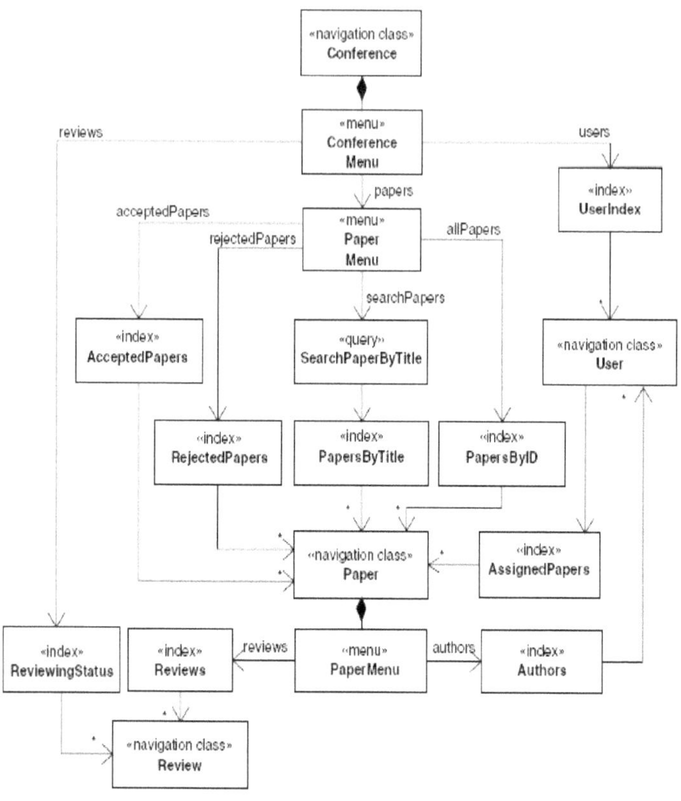

Figure 4.8: Simplified Access Model of the Hypertext Structure Model from Figure 3.7

4.6.4. Relation to Content Modeling

Depending on the underlying modeling method, the hypertext model is more or less strongly dependent on the content model. There exists both a dependence at the type level, e.g., which classes in the content model form which node in the hypertext model, and at the instance level, i.e., which sets of objects in the content model populate that node in the hypertext model. Not all methods describe dependencies between the content model and the hypertext model exactly. Nevertheless, some methods specify a direct derivation of the hypertext from the content by defining nodes on the basis of views (in the sense of "database views") (Schwabe et al. 2002, Koch and Kraus 2002).

4.7. Presentation Modeling

Similar to traditional Software Engineering, presentation modeling deals with the user interface and thus with the look and feel of a Web application. In contrast to traditional applications, the central element of the presentation in Web applications is the page as a visualization unit.

4.7.1. Objectives

Presentation modeling is aimed at designing the structure and behavior of the user interface to ensure that interaction with the Web application is simple and self-explanatory. In addition, the communication and representation task of the Web application are taken into account. Presentation modeling generates a two-fold result: First, it produces a uniform presentation concept by modeling recurring elements on the pages, e.g., headers and footers. It should ideally show the composition of each page and the design of the fields, texts, images, forms, etc., included in these pages. Second, in addition to the structure of the pages, the presentation model describes the behavior-oriented aspects of the user interface, e.g., which button to click to activate a function of the application logic. Due to the wide variety of navigation options and the inherent risk of getting lost, care should be taken to give users appropriate orientation help on the presentation level. This can be achieved, for example, by displaying the current navigation path, or pages visited during the active session.

Not all methods available for modeling Web applications support technology-independent presentation modeling concepts; some rather use technology-specific concepts, such as Stylesheet languages, e.g., XSL (Extensible Stylesheet Language) (Pineda and Kruger" 2003).

Another important factor for Web applications is the graphical layout design of the user interface. It is often produced by a graphic designer based on some basic drawings, or conceptualized by the tool-supported implementation of prototypical pages. Although this task is part of presentation modeling, it is currently not supported by modeling techniques.

4.7.2. Concepts

Model elements are described on three hierarchical levels:

- A *presentation page* describes a page presented to the user as a visualization unit. It can be composed of different presentation units.
- A *presentation unit* serves to group related user interface elements, representing a logical fragment of the page. It presents a node stemming from the hypertext model.

- A *presentation element* is the basic building block of the presentation model. Presentation elements represent a node's set of information and can include text, images, audio, etc.

We can visualize the composition of presentation pages on the basis of a nested UML class diagram representation known as "composition", as in the example shown in Figure 3-9. This example uses the stereotype classes page and presentation unit to depict presentation pages and presentation units. Notice that all types of presentation elements are also designated by appropriate UML stereotypes. Figure 4-9 shows two presentation pages of our reviewing system. A paper is positioned on the page called "PaperPage" with the appropriate fields as well as a link to the paper's full version and a link to display the paper's authors. Moreover, the user can press a button to add a new review. The page "AuthorPage" has two presentation units, i.e., the list of all authors and each author's detailed information.

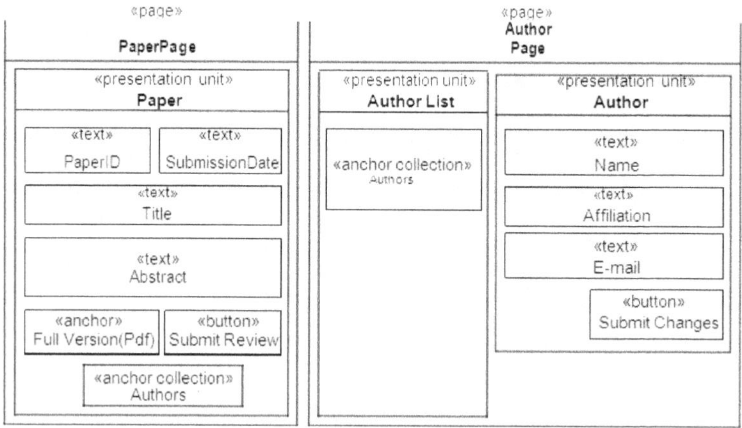

Figure 4.9: Presentation Pages of the Reviewing System

Behavioral aspects of the user interface, such as a reviewer's interaction to navigate to the papers assigned to him or her for reviewing, can be modeled by means of behavior diagrams, as shown in Figures 4-10, 4-11, and 4-12. In general, a user's interaction with the Web application does not only involve the presentation level; it is also forwarded to the hypertext level and the content level, depending on the type of interaction. We can see in the simplified sequence diagrams in Figures 4-11 and 4-12, that a reviewer activates the navigation to the index of assigned papers by using the navigation bar from within the conference home page. This information is, in turn, composed of the relevant papers on the content level. The list allows the user to select a paper out of the list of assigned papers. The user can then navigate to select one paper, which will be displayed in the details view.

4.7.3. *Relation to Hypertext Modeling*

Similarly to mapping the content model to the hypertext model, we also have to specify how hypertext elements should be mapped to presentation elements. This is normally done under the assumption that all instances of a node will be displayed on the presentation level. As mentioned before, the interactions triggered by a user are not necessarily limited to the presentation level only.For this reason, we have to additionally consider their correspondences to the other links. This correspondence may be in the form of objects and application logic on the content level, and for navigation on the hypertext level.

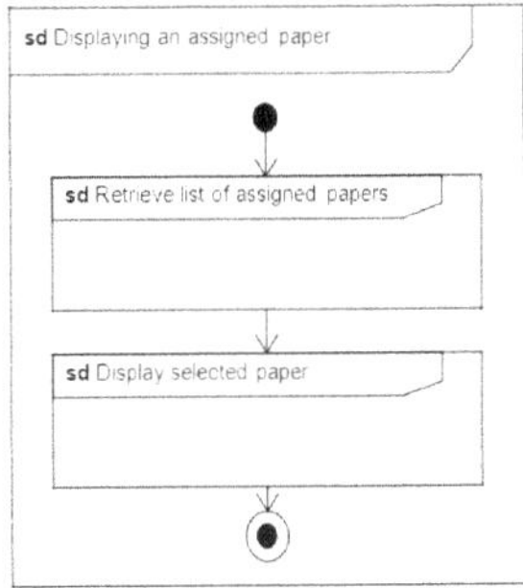

Figure 4.10: Interaction Overview Diagram of the Reviewing System

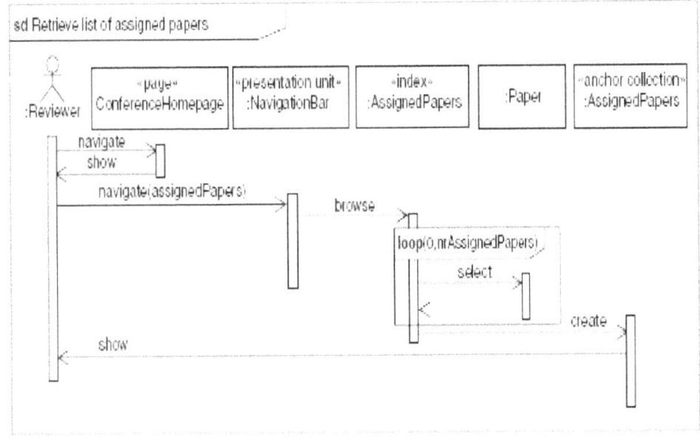

Figure 4.11: Sequence Diagram for Retrieving a List of Assigned Papers

4.8.   Customization Modeling

Since ubiquitous Web applications increasingly gain importance, the consideration of context information and an appropriate adaptation of the application as early as possible in the modeling phase (see also section 1.3.2) are required. Relevant proposals for *customization* originate from the fields of personalization (Kobsa 2001, Brusilovsky 2001) and mobile computing (Eisenstein et al. 2001, Want and Schilit 2001). For a more detailed overview on the origin of customization the reader is referred to (Kappel et al. 2003).

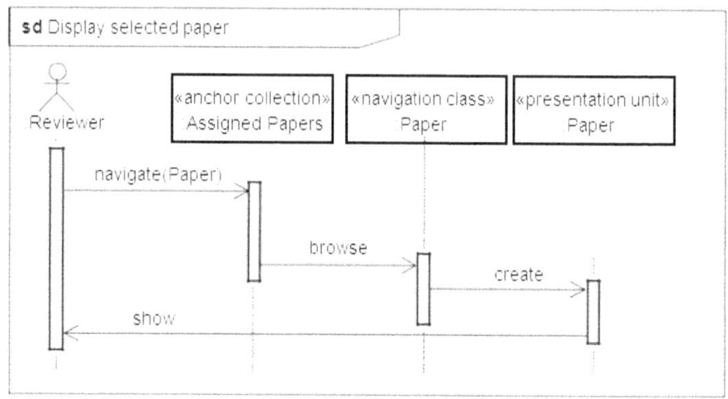

Figure 4.12: Sequence Diagram for Displaying Selected Papers

However, customization modeling is still a very young field, and only a few existing methods for Web application modeling offer a form of customization modeling (Fraternali 1999, Kappel et al. 2000, Ceri et al. 2003, Garrigos' et al. 2005). For the UWE methodology (Baumeister et al. 2005) have recently proposed an aspect-oriented approach to deal with customization.

4.8.1. Objectives

Customization modeling is aimed at explicitly representing *context* information, and the *adaptations* derived from it. Depending on the modeling method the result is not always an explicit customization model. In most cases, customization modeling is intermingled with content, hypertext, and presentation models. Customization has to be distinguished from maintenance or re-engineering. Customization modeling considers context information that can be predicted at modeling time which can assume different values when the Web application is run. In contrast, adaptation due to changes in the organizational or technological environment is part of maintenance or re-engineering activities.

4.8.2. Concepts

Customization requires examining the Web application's usage situation, i.e., dealing with the questions of "what" should be adapted and "when". To be able to personalize a Web application we have to model and manage the preferences and characteristics of a user in a so-called *user profile*. For example, to adapt a Web application in the field of mobile computing, we have to consider *device profiles*, *location information*, and *transmission bandwidth*. This information is then represented within the context model in form of a class diagram. At runtime, context can change, e.g., users change their preferences, or the application is "consumed" at different locations. This situation, in turn, is the reason why we have to adapt the Web application.

With regard to the abstraction level of the context information, one can distinguish between *physical context* and *logical context*. The physical context results from the respective usage situation (e.g., a user's login name or the GSM cell in which a user is currently located). The logical context provides additional context knowledge (e.g., address at work versus address at home, working hours versus spare time). This context information can also be provided to the Web application by external sources. One example of such an external source that provides information for a more detailed specification of the location context are Geographic Information Systems (GIS). Initial approaches, such as the *ContextToolkit* (Abowd 1999) or the *NEXUS* project (Fritsch et al. 2002), have been proposed to support universal components capable of supplying different types of physical and logical context information.

The adaptation to a context can be modeled in either of two fundamentally different ways. First, it can be modeled in a *result oriented* way by creating various models or model variants with regard to the different set of variants of the context information. This approach is known as *static adaptation*. The hypertext modeling example shown in Figure 3-7 describes a statically adapted hypertext structure to the context of the "PC" user role. The drawback of static adaptation is the exponential growth of model variants to be considered. Second, *dynamic adaptation* can be used.

In contrast to static adaptation, dynamic adaptation adds context-dependent transformation rules to the content, hypertext, and presentation models. These transformation rules describe the variants to be created at runtime. For example, dynamic transformation rules, e.g., formulated as ECA (Event/Condition/Action) rules, could specify the addition or removal of model elements, or the filtering of instances, to create a personalized list with papers on the topics a user is interested in. Whether dynamic or static adaptation is the better approach depends on the use case. Dynamic adaptation has the benefit that it avoids the combinatory explosion of model variants. Its drawback is that the result, i.e., the model's variant adapted to the context, is not available directly, but will actually be created "at runtime", which makes it more difficult to understand the model. The reader will find a detailed discussion of proposals for customization modeling in (Kappel et al. 2003).

Figures 4-13 and 4-14 show how the hypertext and presentation levels of the review-ing system example can be dynamically adapted. We use annotations – stereotyped with customization – to add customization rules to the adapted class. The rules described informally in this example can be specified in more detail by using a formal language, e.g., the Object Constraint Language (OCL) (Baerdick et al. 2004), in further refining steps. Figure 4-13 shows an example of how the hypertext structure can be customized so that the papers a user can read are limited to those with topics of interest to that user. The elements of the access structure, "Interesting Papers", are adapted dynamically by transformation rules based on personal topics of interest. The example in Figure 4-14 shows how elements of the presentation model can be adapted by the use of transformation rules. Specifically, the button "Enter Review" should be visible only for users with the "Reviewer" role.

Most of the currently existing methodologies tackle the modeling of customization by defining rules or a filter for each point in the Web application where customization applies as has been shown in the previous examples. A different approach is to consider customization as a cross-cutting concern. UWE follows such an approach using aspect-oriented modeling (AOM) techniques (Baumeister et al. 2005). AOM allows on the one side for a systematic separation of the system functionality from the customization aspects, and on the other side it allows for reduction of redundancy.

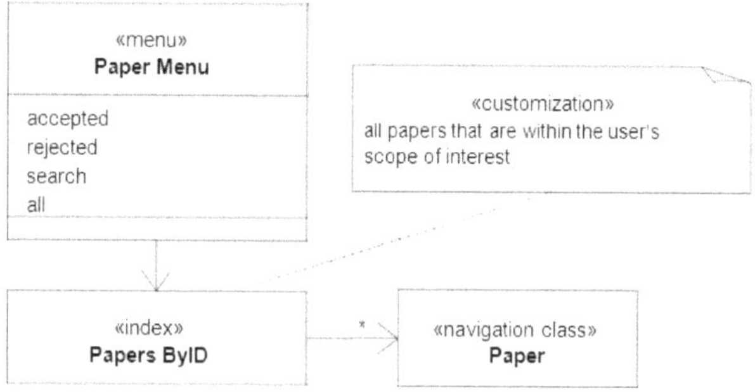

Figure 4.13: Dynamic Adaptation of an Index in the Hypertext Model

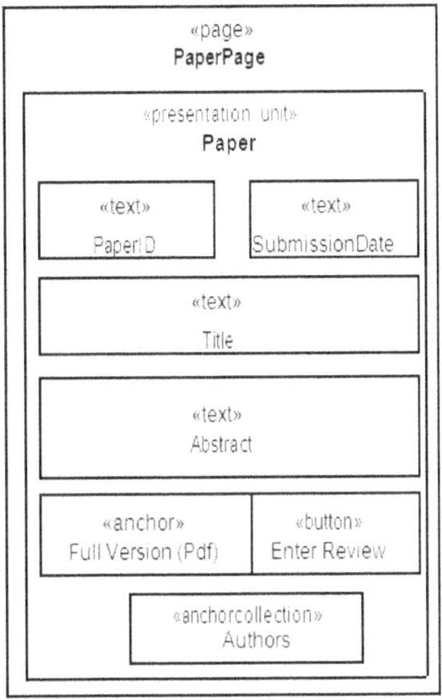

Figure 4.14: Dynamic Adaptation of a Page in the Presentation Model

UWE materializes the cross-cutting concern by the use of stereotyped UML packages for the *pointcut* part and the *advice* part of an aspect. An aspect is a (graphical) statement saying that in addition to the features specified in the principal models, each model element of the package pointcut also has the features specified by the advice. In other words, a complete description including both general system functionality and additional, cross-cutting features is given by the composition – so-called weaving – of the main model and the aspect.

UWE distinguishes between customization at content, hypertext and presentation level (as represented in Figure 4-2).

For example, links can be annotated, sorted, hidden or generated dynamically according to the current status of a user or context model. The approach consists of extending the UWE meta model with a modeling element *NavigationAnnotation* that can be attached to any navigation link (Baumeister et al. 2005). Figure 4-15 shows how the designer used the *NavigationAnnotation* to add an attribute (*PresStyle*) included in the advice part to the set of links included in the pointcut part. Figure 3-16 shows the results of the weaving process.

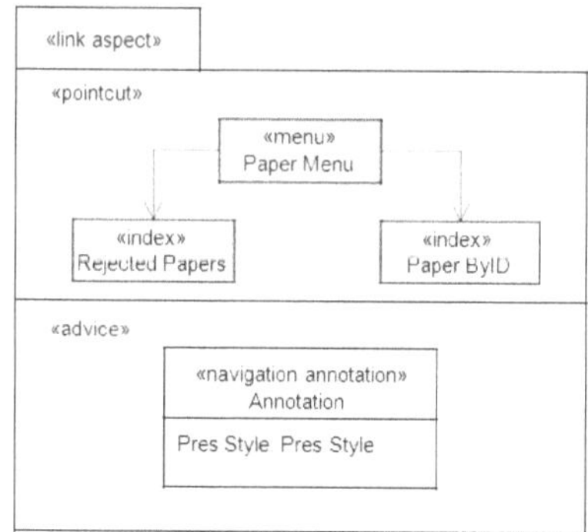

Figure 4.15: Modeling Adaptation with Aspects

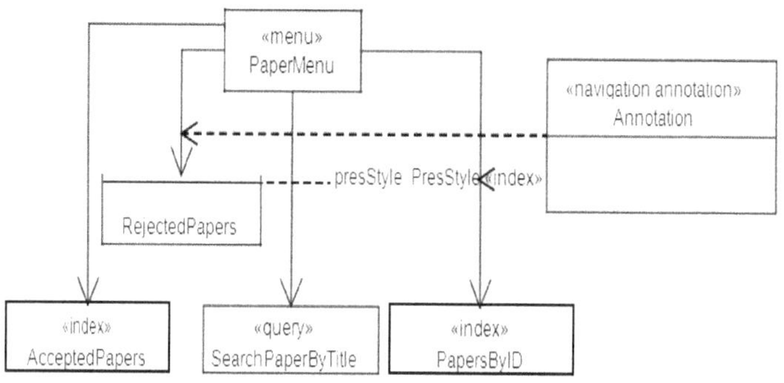

Figure 4.16: Results of the Waving Process

Dynamic customization can be achieved including rules written in OCL in the advice part of the aspect.

4.8.3. *Relation to Content, Hypertext, and Presentation Modeling*

As shown in Figure 3-2, customization can influences all levels of a Web application modeling process. Changes can be limited locally to one level or affect several levels. Separation of the customization model from the content, hypertext, and presentation models are recommended with regard to changeability, flexibility, and encapsulation, but most existing methods do not provide for this separation. And sometimes, as in the reviewing system, such a separation is difficult. For example, the user of a Web application and his or her preferences are context modeling issues, but the user may also be an issue in content modeling, as the reviewing system example shows.

CHAPTER V

TECHNOLOGY-AWARE WEB APPLICATION DESIGN

The Web emerged as an extremely simple hypertext system that supports the concept of global linking. This "simplicity" recipe for success has cast doubt on the use of mature *design methods and tools for hypertext/hypermedia* to the current day. XML was the first technology to make "fully grown" hypertext systems possible, but they are far from being customary. In addition, in the relatively short history of the Web the focus has been on database connections and thus *information design.*

However, information design has been only partially usable for Web application design. The integration of extensive software modules in clients and servers and thus *object-oriented software design* techniques has long been important in the "Web melting pot". However, since all mentioned aspects have remained significant, none of the three roots alone can offer satisfactory solutions. Consequently, approaches for Web-specific design are in demand.

But the "typical" characteristics of Web applications are still so much in a state of flux and the field is so young, that *best practices* and the resulting good design methods, design processes, design notations, and design tools have not really emerged.

This is why, in the current situation, only one approach can be recommended: Web application developers should break down Web applications into three logical layers which, in turn, are split in two halves each by the same principle. We distinguish between *components* (particularly Web application nodes, i.e., media, software components, database accesses), and their arrangement in a *mesh.*

We identify the following three layers: (1) the presentation design, where we design the look and feel, and where multi-modal user interfaces come into play; (2) the interaction design, where we design the navigation by use of meshes, and the specific dialog by use of components; and (3) the functional design, which specifies the "core" of our Web application. As our design becomes more concrete on each level and for both parts (nodes, mesh), we will have to fall back on tools for hypertext, information, and software design. Unfortunately, the current state-of-the-art does not offer satisfactory technical support for the integrative part of our design.

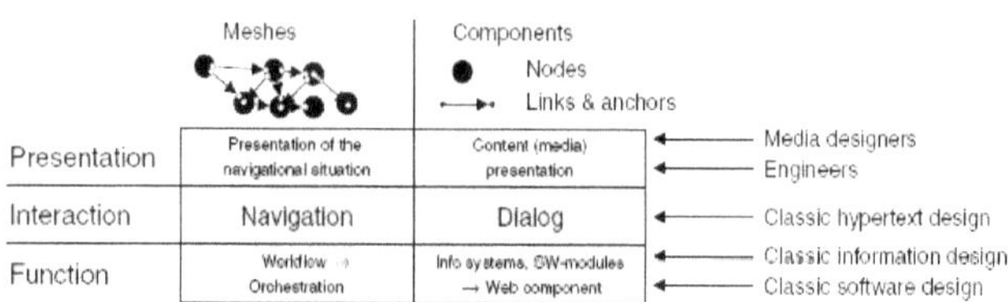

Figure 5.1: Basic Elements of Hypertext Documents

5.1.   Introduction

This chapter represents an introduction to the design of Web applications. But first, we have to shed some light onto common practice. Common practice is characterized by poorly coordinated design tasks, i.e., information design, hypertext design, and software design: section 5.2 will therefore use an evolutionary approach to introduce these parts and discuss possibilities and problems prior to discussing the integration part. The following three sections will try to overcome the uncoordinated clash of several "cultures" by using a three-part structure based on new perspectives; each of these three sections discusses one of the three parts, i.e., presentation design, interaction design, and functional design.

History in Brief

The World Wide Web's first attempts at walking was characterized by document-centric, text-based HTML pages, for which the term "Web application" seems to be exaggerated. In fact, the HTML document description language is rooted in the print and publishing industry. HTML promotes the creation of large, structured documents, which are enriched by links. In addition to its uncompromising simplicity, the WWW secret of success was the full integration of global links – URLs. "Large documents" mean that HTML promotes the *violation* of a maxim in hypertext research, by which hypertext nodes should represent the smallest possible meaning-carrying units. Today, these deficits can be removed only by the XML-based standards of the W3C (http://www.w3c.org), but still partly only "in principle", because improvements are introduced slowly into browsers and Web servers.

The transition to "true" Web applications, together with the development of script languages, e.g., JavaScript (on the browser side), and interfaces like CGI (on the server side), brought interactivity and databases and the dynamic creation of HTML documents into play. And finally, together with the emergence of Java, Web applications started to increasingly gain software character. The classification section in Chapter 1 mentioned this point briefly.

To reflect this large number of different aspects in the design of Web applications, we will use Web application design subtasks, as shown in Figure 5-1, in our further discussion. This discussion will basically distinguish the *components* of Web applications, i.e., the nodes and links that connect them, and their start and destination points within nodes ("anchors"), from the *mesh* consisting of such components, i.e., from the entire Web application. When we say "entire" we realize that the term will have to remain flexible because references to parts of the WWW that are beyond the control of Web application developers should remain possible. This appears to be the only way for the Web to remain *worldwide*.

In addition to the two-part structure mentioned above, Figure 5-1 shows a three-part layering, with a clear differentiation between *presentation* and *interaction*, similar to the Model-View-Controller (MVC) concept and to the way its large number of extensions (Buschmann et al. 1996) distinguish between view and controller. On the one hand, the presentation concerns the *mesh*, taking the node (the "cursor" on the way through the mesh; there might be several in parallel) currently visited by a user into account. On the other hand, the presentation of *components*, i.e., node contents, is a central design task (see Chapter 1); this early stage emphasizes the relevant characteristics of Web applications, particularly content-related characteristics, such as document character and multimediality, and presentation-related characteristics such as aesthetics and self-explanation. This means that it is important to involve experts (called *media designers* in this context) and coordinate them with other Web application developers (called *engineers* in this context).

The separation of meshes from components continues on the interaction level. Interaction within a mesh is normally referred to as *navigation*. Navigation can be explorative, as expressed by the term *browsing*. The user follows links that appear interesting to him or her while reading pages, and moves across the mesh on an apparently random path. Alternatively, navigation can be (co)controlled by – perhaps sophisticated – software, which adapts the selection options in each navigation situation (determined by the "cursor"), e.g., in the form of a dynamically changing navigation bar, or a graph layout with the currently deactivated parts grayed out. Sophisticated user models, domain models, or instructional strategies (in e-learning) could determine these dynamics (De Bra et al. 1999) (Brusilovsky 2001). In contrast, we refer to interaction with components as a *dialog* in the sense of a user interface. In a Web application's first interaction degree, the dialog is implemented by forms (or templates). Together with the possibility to use Java software as components (applets), the wealth of possibilities for graphical user interfaces became available to Web applications for the first time. Ubiquitous Web applications increasingly support the wide range of mobile clients, including voice-based devices, multi-modal dialogs, etc. When designing such systems, the MVC approach mentioned above hits its limits at the component side. Although still valid as an organizational scheme, MVC as a concept does not particularly address the navigational nature of user interface interaction.

Notice a small indication that the horizontal (presentation/interaction) and vertical (meshes/components) separation is justified. Meshes had not been represented at all in the early HTML-based Web, while navigation within a mesh was supported (by clicking links or using the Forward/Back buttons in the browser). Inversely, the presentation of components (HTML documents rendered by the browser) has been taken very seriously since the time when the first graphical browsers had been introduced, while dialog with a component has been possible only since the introduction of "forms" in HTML.

Similar to the MVC concept, where the so-called "model" accommodates the actual core, i.e., an application's functionality, the design principle shown in Figure 5-1 requires an additional layer, referred to as *functional design* in the following discussion. We want the term "function" to initially be neutral and comprise all Web development stages. The early document-centric stage was characterized mainly by static contents, i.e., contents in the form of components specified by authors, so that functions in the true sense were only calls of the presentation or playback function (for media), which means that the layer was virtually empty. In connection with the possibility to access databases, Web applications had increasingly been influenced by the principles of classic information systems and databases, i.e., the design of the functional part consisted essentially of the information design. Together with the transition to the more recent Web application categories mentioned in Chapter 1 (workflow-based, collaborative, portal, ubiquitous), components with extensive functionalities have moved into the foreground. Of course, object-oriented approaches are suitable to integrally model functional and data aspects. Accordingly, Java and competing approaches such as ASP/.NET, had initially played a dominating role. They have more recently been substantially enhanced by W3C standards to strengthen worldwide interoperability in the Web. The growing significance of active components is also reflected in remote procedure calls, e.g., those according to the SOAP standard, appearing in addition to "static" links, and in the fact that a link's destination node can be determined at runtime, e.g., via UDDI. In a time strongly influenced by information systems, the mesh side was characterized by *workflow management* approaches, which are more suitable for static component meshing models in the sense of the steps involved in a business process. Together with the introduction of *Web Services* and concepts to model cross-corporate business processes, more flexible meshing concepts came into play by terms like *orchestration* or *choreography* (W3C 2002a), but the development of these concepts is still underway. The degree of dynamics in ubiquitous Web applications will probably increase in line with the emergence of an open service market. Services will then virtually be Web components, which can be orchestrated to a mesh in the sense of ubiquitous, highly customized and complex Web applications, matching the users' needs.

As a general approach for the design of Web applications, it is recommended to cover all six parts highlighted in Figure 5-1, and to observe the following aspects, in view of our above discussion:

- The cultural background of all developers should be represented in a team, and care should be taken as to their integration.
- There are independent models, methods, and tools for the design and implementation in each of the six parts, but they differ considerably, depending on the Web application category (see Chapter 1). A full discussion of this issue would go beyond the scope and volume of this book. It should be noted, however, that further evolution of a Web application towards a more sophisticated category is conceivable.
- The selection mentioned above not only has to consider the planned Web application categories, but also the planned technologies. This dependence is so strong that it plays a central role in this chapter.
- A comprehensive design process as a path through the six parts shown in Figure 5-1 cannot be generally recommended. Rather, it is meaningful to cover all three horizontal layers first on one side and then on the other, perhaps iteratively. While the mesh side can be designed first when most of a Web applications development is new, we first have to develop reusable components if we have no knowledge of meshes. Within one side, it is recommended from the software engineering perspective to begin on the lowest layer, because interaction can be oriented to the function, and presentation can be oriented to interaction. If aesthetics and other user-related characteristics of Web applications are in the foreground, then the opposite way is recommended.

5.2. Web Design from an Evolutionary Perspective

5.2.1. Background

As mentioned at the beginning of Chapter 1 and above, one central characteristic of Web applications is their document-*centric view*, i.e., a much greater importance of human-readable information versus conventional software: *content is king*. Initially, Tim Berners-Lee wanted to develop the Web to be a simple though worldwide hypertext system via the Internet, and he mainly focused on textual information. Accordingly, the activities of *authors* and *programmers* clash, or blatantly speaking, the world of artists hits that of engineers. This section looks at these opposites through historic spectacles to better understand Web applications and discuss important design issues.

5.2.2. *Information Design: An Authoring Activity*

This section distinguishes between the *era before the Web*, the *HTML era* (from the advent of the Web until 1997), and the current *XML era* (W3C 1998). The beginning of the HTML era was exclusively focused on *authoring*. Only hypertext documents were supported, as the name of the so-called Web programming language, HTML, suggests: *Hypertext Markup Language*, a language for instructions – or tags – strewn throughout text documents. In the course of time, HTML supported other media: images, time-sensitive media, such as video and audio, etc., reflected in the term *hypermedia*, which is sometimes used to distinguish HTML from hypertext and sometimes synonymously to hypertext. We will use hypertext as a generic term in the following discussion.

The *hypertext* concept is older than HTML; its basic idea was formulated by Vannevar Bush as early as at the end of World War II in view of the emerging wealth of technical information carriers. Ted Nelson coined the term itself in the 1960s. Hypertext documents are composed of the following:

- Nodes, links, and anchors, as introduced in Chapter 1.
- Meshes and other aggregates. Meshes designate coherent nodes and links, and were called *hypertext documents* in the era before the Web. Examples for aggregates include views (e.g., for experts and laymen among readers), paths (pre-determined reading sequences), and meta-nodes (meshes that can be embedded in enveloping meshes, like a node). The simple Web of the HTML era didn't support them, but their significance has grown strongly with the advent of advanced modularization concepts, e.g., navigational structures like "star-shaped navigation" (see section 5.4.6), to mention one interaction design example.

Though HTML considered initially only the authoring aspect, it represented a backward step compared with popular hypertext systems even in this respect, and even with regard to the fundamental vision of non-linear explorative documents (see Chapter 1). The Web's popularity was possible only thanks to its simplicity and free worldwide availability. Its major weaknesses are mentioned briefly below in as far as they are relevant from the design perspective:

- HTML can be understood as a (classic) document description language with hypertext tags grafted on. This seduces people to disregard the atomicity principle of nodes; many "HTML" documents (actually nodes) are several pages long, and the basic hypertext idea of non-sequential reading is present only rudimentarily or in exceptional cases.
- HTML mixes orthogonal aspects like hypertext structure (via tags for links and anchors), document structure (headers, lists, etc.), and layout (background color, italics, etc.).
  - Though the Web recognizes the distributed software architecture with browsers and servers introduced in Chapter 3, it lacks the "horizontal" software architecture of abstract machines. Examples include the classic Dexter architecture, which separates the content and mesh management from the presentation, or the layering suggested in Chapter 4 and in this chapter.
  - HTML is text-centric. Other media often occur only as link destinations (dead-end roads); many media types are not supported as link sources at all or have been only recently. It was not until the advent of SMIL that the description of temporal media could be covered on the Web.
  - The Web's evolution increased the significance of first drawback above. The support for structuring and formatting within nodes improved gradually, while important hypertext aspects, e.g., user-definable node and link types, reverse links, separate storage of links and nodes, non-trivial destination anchors, etc., are still missing.

To better understand the authoring aspect of XML, in contrast to the above, we first have a look at HTML's origin. It dates back to SGML, a standardized generic *markup language* for the world of print shops and publishing companies. "Generalized" means that SGML defines valid tags and rules to be used for an entire class of documents (i.e., a specific field of application and the documents it normally uses). The results are *document type definitions* (*DTDs*). An SGML parser can read DTDs and check documents to see whether or not they correspond to a DTD. However, special software has to be written to interpret and execute the instructions specified by tags. Publishing companies use DTDs to distinguish between different book, magazine, and brochure formats, forms, and many other things. In the beginning, HTML was nothing but an SGML-DTD for the "screen" format, extended by tags for links and anchors as "grafted on" hypertext functionalities. Later HTML versions corresponded to new DTDs. Browsers of the HTML era are not SGML parsers; instead, they have support for a few DTDs (the supported

HTML versions) hardcoded into them, including the way they interpret tags and translate commands. The "rendering" is also hardcoded and only the introduction of *CSS* (*cascading style sheets*) enabled reusable layouts and a rudimentary way of separating the layout from the structure.

The XML era dawned when standard PCs were ready to "digest" SGML parsers. It almost suggested itself to standardize a simplified version of SGML to make the wealth of possibilities of a generic markup language usable. Together with the emergence of XML, an enormous number of "simple programming languages", defined as XML-DTDs (more recently called *XML schemas*), had been defined, including a language to describe remote procedure calls (SOAP), a language to describe financial transactions (XML-EDI), a counterpart to HTML (XHTML), and many more.

Since XML lets you formally describe the syntax but not the semantics, modern browsers can *parse* arbitrary XML schemas and documents, but they (essentially) can *execute* only XHTML.

Almost all the weaknesses of HTML mentioned above have meanwhile been addressed in various XML standards. Whether and how these partly competing standards will proliferate remains to be seen.

We can identify a few basic rules for the *design* of document-based Web applications, i.e., for the authoring aspect, from the above discussion:

- Meshes should form the center of information design.
- Conventional documents should be decomposed into atomic nodes.
- Aspects such as layout and content, node and mesh, etc., should be separated conceptually, even if a technology doesn't support such a separation.
- The selected technology should support advanced concepts, e.g., central link management, at least in the design, ideally also in the content management system (hidden from the end-user), and in intranets even in the implementation technology itself. XML-based solutions should be given preference over proprietary approaches.

5.2.3. *Software Design: A Programming Activity*

This section continues to take a historical perspective by distinguishing between the gradual development of the "programmable Web" and the development of (distributed) programming.

Programmable Web

The first steps towards "dynamics" were HTML forms. With their introduction, the significance of script languages increased dramatically, since they could be tailored specifically to the processing needs of browsers or servers and were easy to handle. Scripts are generally used to create HTML pages on the fly, depending on inputs in an HTML form.

Regardless of the language used to create new HTML pages, the script or program should offer pre-defined data structures and operations to be able to create typical HTML page elements, such as headers of different levels, paragraphs, lists, and other things, fill them with contents, and put it all together (as a tree-type structure of elements). This is virtually always based on the *Document Object Model* (*DOM*), which has been defined consistently as new HTML versions came along over the years, and which is available in script languages or programming languages.

The Java developers originally set out to introduce "the language of the Web" with the idea that browsers should *represent* not only HTML, but also *run* Java. Similar to HTML documents, so-called *Java applets* were designed for download from servers, and instead of a static document, a program's (applet) user interface would appear in the browser window. Accordingly, the main focus was placed on security aspects to prevent third-party applets from executing undesired operations on end-users' machines.

With Java, Sun had the vision of a *pay-per-use* software market, which has hardly been realized today. However, Java itself became very popular, albeit only to a moderate extent as an applet programming language, but instead as a "regular" programming language and a language for servers and distributed programming. Apart from scripts and applets, browsers run programs particularly for dynamic representation of multimedia presentations, for example those developed with Macromedia Flash.

Distributed Programming

Distributed programs in the Internet originally ran directly on top of TCP connections; *inter-process communication* (*IPC* for short), i.e., the exchange of messages between two equal peers, dominated. For multimedia, IPC (enhanced by guaranteed quality of service for "streams") appears to have regained some significance, but had been replaced by *Remote Procedure Call* (*RPC*), accompanied by client/server architectures in the 1990s. The next evolutionary step, i.e., the adaptation of RPC to object-oriented programming languages, was incorrectly referred to as "distributed object-oriented programming" and eventually led to further proliferation of distributed programs, with technologies like CORBA and Java's *Remote*

Method Invocation (*RMI*). The above name is incorrect because object-oriented prin-ciples, such as modularity and flexibility, contradict the RPC world of monolithic clients and servers, which continue to exist in CORBA and RMI. The kind of distributed object-oriented programming that would deserve this name has been stuck in the academic stage till today. Instead, *event-based communication* (*EBC* for short), and publish/subscribe archi-tectures have become increasingly important. In EBC the information creator determines when to communicate ("when a new event occurs") using the push principle in con-trast to the pull principle where the requester initiates the communication. Clients register event types they are interested in via *subscription*. These event types, rather than the con-nections, determine the group of receivers. Receivers originally not included in a group can be added easily. JavaBeans and *message-oriented middleware* use rudimentary forms of EBC.

The strong trend towards software-centric Web applications led to a situation where the developments mentioned above have occurred in time-lapse (cf. e.g. the emergence of Web Services).

5.2.4. *Merging Information Design and Software Design*

Object-oriented software development meaningfully encapsulates coherent data together with the pertaining operations – the methods. Puristic approaches would not even let you access data directly from the outside; only the methods are "visible" to object users. Obviously, meshes consisting of objects and the call relationships between them are very similar to node – link meshes in hypertext. On the one hand, a hypertext node could be thought of as an object with methods, e.g. "present human-readable data", "select anchor", and "follow link to selected anchor". On the other hand, buttons in HTML forms often hide JavaScript methods. So, investing some time and effort, we could implement many general object-oriented software designs as HTML documents. After all, applets are Java objects *and* hypertext nodes by definition. The fact that object orientation and hypertext have been blending can easily be seen in a node of the type "computer-generated video". Just think of a link pointing from a Web page to a comic's animation. If you follow this link, the animation is played but you may or may not know whether the images are played out from one single file, like in a video, or calculated by a program in real time, i.e., whether you see a video document or a video program. But then, do we really need to distinguish between the roles of authors and programmers? We are inclined to say *No*, but there are still very few Web developers who represent both "cultures".

Obviously, neither have the Web and distributed programming technologies fully merged, nor have the "cultures" of humans involved in Web application development. However, it might be useful to simply ignore an artificial "technology-driven" separation of the object world from the hypertext world in a design process. We would then design Web applications from elements (object – node hermaphrodites) and links (which could also be method call relationships). This approach lets us identify technologies to be used later on, or from case to case. The following greatly simplified alternatives should be observed in this approach:

- *Elements* can be implemented as either static, client-generated pages (e.g., JavaScript), or as server-generated pages (ASP, JSP). In addition, they can be implemented as applets, user interfaces of distributed object-oriented programs (Java), or static or generated media. What users see in their browser can be media contents, forms, or software user interfaces, depending on the characteristic of the presented (rendered) HTML. Things that users can select, click, and run are *links*.

- *Links* stand for URLs in HTML, or for XLinks in XML, if the target is information rather than a program, and if both the content and the address are known at time of implementation (plain HTML) or at presentation time (dynamic HTML). Otherwise, links represent remote calls to, for example, remote scripts (if information has to be "calculated"), or methods (if the calculations required are algorithmic). If the destination *address* is to be calculated on the fly, then the software technique used should support dynamically calculated object links (this is possible even in HTML with some workarounds, i.e., by installing proxies between the browser and the server, and by implementing the pointer re-direct concept).

5.2.5. *Problems and Restrictions in Integrated Web Design*

The road towards the integration of hypertext, information, and software design into Web design is bumpy, particularly due to three specific obstacles: "cultural", technological, and conceptual problems. On the "cultural" side, we could criticize that mutual understanding for clashing cultures is insufficient not only among Web developers in practice, but also among researchers, tool and method developers, and trainers. On the technological side, the available tools and methods are insufficient. On the conceptual side, the integrated concept drawn there would really have to be adapted to latest developments and findings before it can reach the maturity needed to be implemented in tools and methods, or even proliferate. However, this should not prevent good Web developers from adapting the outlined model to their needs, and using it in their Web designs, at least conceptually. These developers could then select tools that allow them to map the model to a machine-readable design, at least rudimentarily.

We will now briefly discuss the three problems mentioned above to better understand them; a detailed discussion would go beyond the scope and volume of this book. *Cultural* obstacles can have so many faces that we want to give just one representative example: while graphical design specifics of Web pages are dealt with in textbooks and educational material, information design specifics for the Web are hardly addressed as an educational issue. Examples of *technological* obstacles are easier to look at in more detail:

- The design of Web pages in the sense of information design and software design and the subsequent development phases are normally *not* supported by the technologies available on the market.

- The transition from forms-based interactive user interfaces to software with graphical user interfaces normally represents a dramatic technological change, because Java applets have not gained much ground in the world of industrial software production, even though Java has become a much more general "programming language for the Web" than initially expected, e.g., in the form of Java Server Pages (JSPs).

- There is no appropriate technology for some desirable variants of the two design concepts outlined in section 5.2.4, i.e., *elements* and *links*. For example, HTML has no way of calculating a link's destination at navigation time (when it is clicked), except for using intermediate proxies, which is somewhat cumbersome.

- The fine-grained mixture of the authoring and programming aspects within an element or a link is not sufficiently supported by technologies. For example, if we want to support sophisticated navigation across a mesh, we would have to implement a separate navigation software layer in HTML or XML and introduce it on top of the mesh. The only way we could currently achieve this is by putting in a lot of development work, using special XML-based technologies that are still scarcely used in practice.

As far as the third and last problem is concerned, i.e., *conceptual* obstacles, we have to emphasize particularly the issue of sustainability and reusability. This issue will be discussed in section 5.6.

5.2.6. *A Proposed Structural Approach*

We will repeatedly have to distinguish between hypertext design, information design, and software design in the following sections, because, unfortunately, this is still customary in design methods and design tools, and in practice. However, we will try to avoid it in favor of an integrative view of Web application design.. To recall the three parts, we list them below, each with a component side and a mesh side:

- *Presentation design*: This design has the output of documents, media, and data (in the sense of an information system, or in the sense of application data of a software component) on its component side. On its mesh side, this design should focus on the visualization, auditory or multi-modal output of meshes, and the component(s) currently visited by a user. Since this side is still in the research stage, apart from the common use of navigation bars in browsers, it will be discussed only briefly in section 5.3.

- *Interaction design*: This part is concerned with the control flow of a user's interaction with a Web application. On the mesh side, the term *navigation* has become customary, while the term *dialog* is used on the component side. Both issues will be discussed in section 5.4.

Functional design: Section 5.5 introduces the core design of components and meshes, emphasizing the software developer's perspective, because this is important for the latest categories of Web applications (see Chapter 1). Accordingly, the component side will be described as an information design, rather than a software components' design. Similarly, the mesh side will focus on the composition of active components into business processes (workflows) and highly customized ubiquitous Web applications.

5.3. Presentation Design

In a presentation design, "media designers" (see section 5.1) define the look and – to some extent – the structure of how multimedia contents are presented. Based on the original idea that *content is king*, classic HTML specified contents together with format instructions, links, and programs (scripts). In contrast, modern presentation design follows the conceptual separation of a Web application's content and its presentation. The content of a Web application results from the composition of explicitly developed multimedia contents on the component side and implicitly defined contents on the mesh side. This means that a good presentation design allows us to flexibly adapt the presentation to various cultural, technological, and contextual requirements.

In addition, many Web pages, Web applications and entire Web sites are restructured or fitted with a new visual design (see Chapter 1) during their lifecycles. In traditional Web development, this often means that hundreds or even thousands of HTML documents have to be adapted manually. The people involved in this HTML document modification process normally need to have sound HTML knowledge. Though suitable tools can be used to some extent, often a considerable part remains to be modified manually. This means that it is either impossible or very costly to consistently model all contents in a larger development team.

Tools available to create Web applications can be grouped into two categories by how they support the presentation design: conventional *page editors* and more advanced *content management systems.*

Page editors are generally used to create smaller ad-hoc Internet presences. Their major benefits are that they are similar to standard software, which lets users work in a familiar environment, and that they allow to directly format contents. Their major drawbacks are that HTML knowledge is necessary for non-trivial tasks, and that developers work on page level, which means that they can easily lose the bigger conceptual picture. Moreover, layout, navigation, and interaction are mixed, which can be considered a simplification for trivial applications only.

In contrast to page editors, *content management systems* allow separating the editorial activities from the layout, facilitating the maintenance of an Internet presence. This means, however, that the structure of an Internet presentation has to be mapped. The specifics of content management systems are that special tools for various participating roles, e.g., graphic artists or editors, are available, while HTML knowledge is normally not required. Another benefit is that content, layout, and navigation are separate, the contents of single information units are specified, and workflows can be mapped. The differentiation between page editors and content management systems introduced here blurs continually, because in recent versions many page editors integrate simple content management system functions.

5.3.1. *Presentation of Nodes and Meshes*

A Web page's content results from the composition of explicitly developed multimedia contents on the component side and implicitly defined contents on the mesh side (e.g., navigation options).

When creating multimedia contents, developers have a large number of design options at their disposal. With regard to the desired concept of separation of content and presentation, these design options are often competing. For example, it generally happens that the flexibility to adapt the content to a presentation context decreases as the number of formatting options increases. For a simple example, let's assume that the HTML elements <b> and <strong> were specified to format text in bold. The <b> format is normally lost on devices that do not support bold presentation, because no alternative was specified. XHTML 2.0 replaces the <b> element by the <strong> element. The presentation of this element is controlled in the presentation design, so that it can be adapted to the technical capabilities of a device, e.g., by using underline if bold is not supported.

While the developer specifies the fundamental look of multimedia contents on the component side, on the mesh side the interaction and functional design implicitly result in unformatted contents.

As an example of tasks involved in the navigation design, let's look at a presentation design for navigation interfaces. Navigation interfaces should help to find answers to three important navigational questions: (1) Where am I? (2) Where was I? and (3) Where can I go?

A presentation design is a typical example of tasks for which experienced knowledge is more important and more feasible than formal methods. *Design patterns* are suitable for such tasks (Rossi et al. 1999). For example, we could fall back on the Use pattern to find answers to the above questions.

The question "Where am I?" can often be answered by using the "breadcrumbs" navigational scheme, based on the Hansel and Gretel fairytale. In a user interface involving navigation through data or pages, breadcrumbs can be a useful mechanism for retracing steps, leaving a visual trail of the path taken. At any point, the user can retrace his or her steps to any previous point visited.

Finding an answer to the question "Where was I?" is not that easy, because HTTP as a core Web technology is a stateless protocol, and linking techniques are primitive. The "Back" button and lists of pages previously visited are generally used in browsers. This simple example shows that there is a need to coordinate the presentation and interaction design. When buying articles on the Web, for example, a user cannot use the "Back" button to undo a purchase, and the corresponding confusion among users is normally avoided only in a few well-designed Web applications. Another important example is consistency, ideally across the entire Web. Different presentations of previously visited links and links not yet visited are a common concept for presentation designs. Jakob Nielsen recommends not changing the usual link colors because, in this respect, consistency should have priority over aesthetics (Nielsen 1997a).

A popular approach to answer the question "Where can I go?" consists in listing all top levels of a Web site. In connection with the "breadcrumbs" navigation scheme and suitable marking of the destinations that can be reached from within the current page, the user basically obtains sufficient information about his or her position within the mesh. As a minimum, this marking should emphasize links in the text (or in another medium); in addition, marking in the navigation bar is recommended. The graphical representation of the mesh and the current position within it is desirable, but it is rarely used in practice due to a lack of standards or generally accepted methods and presentations.

5.3.2. Device-independent Development Approaches

Enhanced requirements on the presentation design result from an increasing demand to consider the trend towards a large number of different Web-enabled devices in the design of Web applications.

The spectrum of these Web-enabled devices includes almost all conceivable classes of mobile devices, from very small mobile phones with WAP browsers over smart phones and organizers to tablet PCs with touch-sensitive displays. Cooperative and very large devices are currently not relevant in practice. When looking at the technical features of mobile devices, a very different set of presentation and interaction options results for use in Web applications.

The presentation design considers these requirements within the scope of special activities to support the device-independent development of applications. For example, the *Device Independent Working Group* (DIWG) (W3C 2001c) of the W3C is currently working on this issue. The tasks of the DIWG include aspects from the field of application development, the adaptation of applications to the user's context, and different representations of information.

5.4. Interaction Design

Interaction design concerns the intersection of the visual, dynamic, functional, and technical elements of Web applications. Its major purpose is to combine these elements and smooth conflicts between them, in order to offer the users an interesting and attractive as well as consistent and easy-to-understand experience. This section suggests a systematic approach that divides the interaction of Web applications into four aspects: user interaction, user interface organization, navigation, and user activities.

5.4.1. User Interaction

Many so-called "Web-enabling" features in legacy systems or applications have a common development approach: the interaction design is reduced to the presentation design. This means that applications are being published on the Web by simply translating their views into HTML pages, while introducing only few additional features, such as concurrent access to databases.

As web applications became more sophisticated, an increasing number of roles were coupled into HTML: information transport, layout, user interaction, navigation, processes (as a by-product of subsequent link traversal), and direct access to digital content. Along with the increasing responsibilities, HTML also evolved packing more functionality to accommodate increasingly complex scenarios. In this process, user interaction became a major limitation: servers need to generate a new page each time, applications run more slowly, and since forms are not sufficient to cover more advanced user interaction techniques, HTML as an interface quickly fell short compared with desktop applications. To overcome these limitations, over the years several technological approaches were developed, with a large set of overlapping functionality that makes it difficult to determine what combination may suit better the particular needs of the application to be developed.

Two opposite forces lie at the heart of the problem: how much interface functionality do we need in order to display the data and perform operations; and secondly, how data-intensive is the application at all (see Figure 5-2). The obvious trade-offs are portability, technology vendor (in) dependence and user (customer) satisfaction.

We will outline a criterion to help organize the development decisions to be made by returning to the core properties of a software application: maintainability, reusability, scalability, sustainability and expandability (Carnegie Mellon Software Engineering Institute 2005) (see Table 5-1).

- *Maintainability* refers to the average effort to locate and fix a software failure, and is usually measured by the simplicity, conciseness, modularity and self-descriptiveness. Web .These user interfaces usually have presentation, data and logic tightly coupled, resulting in difficulties in development and maintenance. On the other hand, there are alternatives such as DHTML and Portlets that, due to a stricter separation of concerns, allow a higher modularity and overall maintainability

- *Reusability* refers to the possibility of factoring out code of a particular application for use in other applications without (many) changes. Development technologies provide different reuse mechanisms such as code/scripting libraries. As the first web pages need to be quickly generated, the need to look for reusability at user interface level is often neglected.

- *Scalability* refers not only to the capability of sustaining larger amounts of users but also, from a development point of view, to the ability of discerning different development activities that can be carried out in parallel by a development team. Some ActiveX-based technologies enable astonishing functionality, however, for larger projects, their atomic nature and level of coupling of development concerns makes it very difficult for a group of developers to be working in the same application simultaneously. XML-based technologies (XHTML, XSL/T) are more scalable from the development point of view, since applications can be structured into different, separated XML standards that map more naturally onto different roles in a development or group.

Finally, we also considered the *expandability* of a system, that is, the degree of effort required to improve or modify software functions' efficiency, and the *sustainability.*

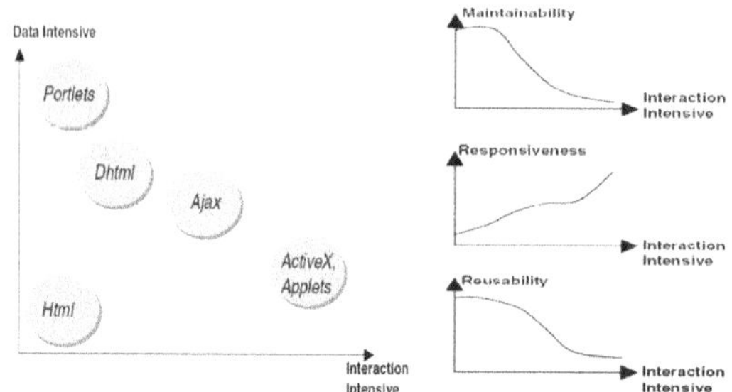

Figure 5.2: Comparison of the Main Interface Development Technologies

Table 5.1: Implementation Alternatives for Web Application User Interfaces

	ActiveX, Applets	AJAX	DHTML	HTML	Portlets
Maintainability	Low	Low	Medium	Low	High
Reusability	Low	Low	High	Low	High
Scalability	Low	Medium	High	High	High
Expandability	Low	Low	High	Low	Medium
Sustainability	Medium	Low	Medium	High	Medium

5.4.2. *User Interface Organization*

By its nature, the aspect discussed here is closely related to the presentation design, but it is determined by integration aspects rather than by presentation aspects. A Web application's user interface often has to represent a large amount of information, operations on this information and relationships between this information. The challenge is then to suitably map this large number of aspects. As a first step towards solving this problem, we can group the elements into interaction channels. This grouping must be clear and consistent across the entire interface. Most of the input and interaction group should remain the same during a session, while the output group generally changes.

A frequent problem occurs when a node contains more information than fits on a screen. When we try to weigh the presentation design aspects against the interaction design aspects, we could let ourselves be guided by the following questions: Should the screen dimensions have priority over the concept that nodes are atomic units (and navigation units)? Should or can a node be split into several smaller nodes? Can additional navigation be an alternative to scrolling? How should complex behavior of the user interface and portability be balanced against each other? As in the previous section, the particular technology blend has implications, this time in terms of navigational semantics (whether navigation is triggered to continue reading or, instead, to access a related topic), portability and usability. We can differentiate different approaches (see Table 5-2):

1. The entire node is sent to the user as HTML. The HTML page includes either scripts or a custom plug-in technology to let the user access subsets of the information. The use of embedded programming avoids further, unnecessary navigation.
2. The entire node is sent to the user as one large HTML page without scripts. The user selects relative links on the page to navigate in the page.
3. A partial view to the node is sent to the user. This page shows meaningfully arranged subsets of information. The user can navigate to other pages to fully read the desired information.

Table 5.2: Implementation Alternatives for Nodes

Implementation approaches	Navigation Semantics	Portability	Usability
HTML + scripting	+	−	+
HTML + relative links	+	+	−
Linked HTML pages	−	+	−

The table shows how different implemen-tation approaches have a positive or negative impact on navigation semantics, portability and usability. Linked pages avoid to overly use scrolling but they lead to additional navigation and, consequently, to larger latency when retrieving the same information again. User studies recommend preferring scrolling over additional steps of navigation (Nielsen 1997a), however, we have mentioned the violation of the hypertext concept of atomic nodes in section 5.2.1. An aggregate concept (missing in HTML, as criticized before) could help us to take both claims into account.

Generally accepted rules for balancing "design forces" against each other normally fail due to the strong influence of Web application specifics. For example, intranet applications might make assumptions about the used browsers. In contrast, e-commerce providers have to focus on portability to make sure all potential customers can access their pages.

5.4.3. Navigation Design

The result from a navigation design is two-fold: the elements users can access on the one hand, and the navigational structure on the other hand. Elements become nodes in the simplest case. The structure defines the relationships between nodes. These relationships will later become visible link anchors in the user interface. In this scenario, the interaction design defines the aspects required for the navigation itself (anchor and URL), and elements required for the users to orient themselves.

5.4.4. Designing a Link Representation: The Anchor

Anchors are visible correspondences of URLs and as such, have to convey both the motivations for users to activate them and the possible consequences. Since the HTML-based implementation of the Web mixes the anchor concept with the link concept into one single unidirectional element, <a>, the semantics melt accordingly. This is the reason why users cannot be sure what the possible consequences will be when following a link (see Table 5-3).

Table 5.3: Possible Consequences when Following a Link

Link Semantics	Uncertainty about its meaning
Navigation	Does the link represent one single destination or several destinations? Is the destination within the current Web site or outside? Is the new node represented in the same window or in a new one? Does the text in the current page change instead of using true navigation?
Download	Which type of document is downloaded? Are tools (e.g., plug-ins) required to represent the document available?
Process	Will the link trigger an action in the server? Will it be possible to navigate back, or to undo the action?

The text of an anchor should ideally be self-explanatory (W3C 2001c). It is also helpful to classify links by categories. In addition, icons can be used inside anchors to visualize links. While such anchors and icons can be specified statically, properties that change dynamically (e.g., whether or not certain media types can be opened) should be marked by using scripts embedded in these pages.

5.4.5. Designing Link Internals: The URL

Navigation processes are triggered by activating anchors in the user interface. These anchors represent links (URLs in HTML) specifying the destination the navigation process should lead to. Anchors should, therefore, be clear, concise, long-lived, and point to an absolute address.

The introduction of XML meant a large progressive step for links and anchors. Combined XML standards like XPath, XPointer, and XLink, offer an infrastructure for general hypermedia functionality, reaching far beyond HTML links.

Overall, it is important for Web application designers to know the expanded capabilities of links in XML. For example, so-called *multidirectional links* can be used to link an XML document with several resources. This means that one single integrated link ties these resources, so that they can be reached in any sequence. For example, a link in an index could point to all occurrences of the words "Web Engineering". Users could then browse these occurrences arbitrarily and use the same link to jump back to the original text. In addition, XML links are self-descriptive, which means that a link can contain arbitrary text that describes the resources it points to.

Since XLink supports both external and internal links, this technology facilitates the introduction and cooperative use of link databases. The enormous number of links in the global Internet creates the desire to efficiently and jointly uses these links. XLink has a feature to define relevant link databases for documents. Additional features (subscriptions or profiles) to make links available in general have increasingly been proposed.

5.4.6. *Navigation and Orientation*

Navigation tools should help to limit the cognitive stress for users. We identify three basic strategies to achieve this goal:

- *Navigation organization*: This strategy determines the entire navigational structure.
- *Orientation aid*: This strategy addresses the questions "Where am I?" and "Where was I?" under interaction aspects of the presentation design, as discussed in section 5.3.1.
- *Link perception*: This strategy concerns mainly issues related to the association of links to motivation and consequence, as discussed in section 5.4.3.

It is obvious that this section has to discuss mainly the first point, which hasn't yet been addressed. It concerns the meaningful organization of the navigation space in a design, including support of meaningful navigation activities, e.g., by avoiding navigation redundancy. One example of redundancies is an index (as list of a search result, or as access structures), where the only way for users to access index elements is by stepping back to the index. This type of navigation is called *star-shaped navigation*. Even the possibility to let users navigate back to the previous element and forward to the next element without having to first return to the index would be a minor improvement. This improvement alone would cut the number of average navigation steps (number of links to be followed) to about half.

As the size of a Web application increases, users profit increasingly from additional orientation and navigation aids. To mention one example, let's look at an object, which is always active and perceivable, and which serves as an index for further navigation objects (nodes and sub-indexes). This *active reference object*, including representations of destination objects, remains visible, helping users either to view destination objects or to select related objects. With regard to reverse navigation, not only is information about the path to the current position made available, but also abbreviations to indexes and nodes along that path.

5.4.7. *Structured Dialog for Complex Activities*

When designing complex Web applications, we often have to make extensive processes that users should activate visible. "Extensive" can mean that an activity extends over several pages. In this case, we can identify three categories of forward navigation: (1) An action is triggered as a result of the navigation step. (2) The navigation calls "only" one additional page, e.g., page 2 of a form. (3) The navigation step leads to a node not directly involved in the activity (additional information, etc.). These alternatives jeopardize both the clarity for the user and the consistency of supported activities. One example is the last step of an activity, which seals binding agreements between a user and a Web application, the so-called *checkout*. If a user decides to move to an independent page prior to completing the checkout, then we have to clarify the state the activity is in. The same is true when a user presses the "Back" button before the checkout is completed.

These problems show that, from the interaction perspective, the characteristics of a business process differ strongly from those of a hypertext application. Table 5-4 summarizes these characteristics.

Table 5.4: Differences between Hypertext and Business Processes

	Hypertext	**Business Process**
Control	The user controls the sequence of pages visited. The next page is called by following a link.	The process defines the next activity within a sequence. Activities are executed sequentially, but the control flow can be complex.
Leaving a page/activity	The user leaves a page by selecting an anchor. The state of this page does not change. A page cannot be ended.	When an activity is left, then it should be clear whether or not it has been completed or interrupted or aborted. The concept of ending activities is an important part of business processes.
Reassume/undo	Returning to a page (e.g., by selecting "Back" in the browser) means merely that the page is called again.	Returning to an activity means that the state that prevailed when the activity was interrupted is reassumed. An explicit call is required to undo an activity.

Approaches to implement business processes in Web applications range from simple HTML (processes are a navigation by-product) to methods and tools for workflow management (*workflow-driven hypertext*). In the second case, workflow interactions are generally not mapped to a Web application's navigation system in an automated way. Process definitions generally describe how processes are embedded in workflows, but not how users interact with processes. Therefore, the interaction design should try to map complex tasks by cleverly using the navigation possibilities.

5.4.8. *Interplay with Technology and Architecture*

We have emphasized repeatedly that design, architecture, and technology are closely related in Web application development. This concerns particularly the transition from simple to complex activities. This transition has an impact on the technology and software architecture of our choice, sometimes being a harsh transition to more complex architectures and better performing technologies as our Web application evolves.

Simple activities that retrieve information can be implemented by simple "3-layer architectures", which use *templates* to generate HTML outputs matching client requests (e.g., based on ASP.NET, JSP, or PHP). In such simple architectures, the application control and the application logics are embedded in the script source code of the templates.

As the information to be represented becomes more complex, for instance, when it is combined from several sources, scripts can become extremely large. It would then be better to replace script languages by user-defined *server-side tags*. These tags allow separating and hiding the code required for representation from the HTML page. However, even if we separate HTML from the code, the control logic in user-defined tags is still implemented separately for each node. Each of them determines the subsequent view independently and forwards it to the appropriate template. This concept can be compared to the use of go-to commands in early programming. The drawbacks of this concept with regard to maintainability, understandability, and modularization were criticized in the 1960s. We can try to overcome "go-to programming" by adopting a basic software engineering notion for complex interactive software products, i.e., using the *Model-View-Controller* (*MVC*) architecture (Krasner and Pope 1988) discussed in Chapter 3.

For complex business processes, however, the MVC concept hits its limits. It does not support transactions that require more than one user input. Consequently, such transactions cannot extend over more than one node (one page, one action). This means that the concept has to be broken down, "banning" complex transactions into the application logic (model). In general, the role of the controller in "Model-2" Web applications is rather underdeveloped. The controller receives events from users and maps them to matching calls. Technological examples of event-call mapping are the XML-based configuration files in *Apache Struts* (http://jakarta.apache.org/struts/).

Manufacturers also brand too simple *controller* concepts as the source of additional complexity and redundancy in code (Sun Microsystems 2003c, Microsoft 2003). A good example is the well-known problem that recurring parameters per page (node) in request messages have to be authenticated, validated, and processed separately. However, different conclusions are derived from this situation.

In its *J2EE Architecture Blueprints*, Sun favors more specialized controllers, separated into two parts: a FrontController and a ViewDispatcher. .NET utilizes the inheritance concept in ASP.NET to group the common behavior of all controllers into one joint Page Controller, which is positioned at the top of the hierarchy.

5.5. Functional Design

The functional design will also have to weigh technological aspects that have a strong impact on the Web application under development. We have to observe the commensurability of our means, but our applications should be expandable, scalable, and maintainable, among other things. Particular difficulties are seen in the interplay of components. Web applications like *news tickers* can normally do without transaction support, while *online shops* may have to map many product phases, from configuration over ordering to repair. This requires transaction and workflow support and the integration of legacy databases and software systems. Chapter 3 discussed appropriate approaches in connection with *Enterprise Application Integration (EAI)*.

5.5.1. *Integration*

We can integrate systems on three levels, which are to be interpreted as sub-levels of the functional design: the data level, the application level, and the process level.

In integration on the *data level*, we make sure that the data between the representations of different applications are transformed and copied.

Examples include primitive transformation steps between the data export from one application and the data import into another application, or the use of JDBC to link databases. This approach doesn't involve the applications themselves, and it doesn't let us validate the data.

In integration on the *application level* (also called *object level*), the interplay occurs over APIs, which means that time and semantics are closely interleaved. However, many details depend on the middleware used for coupling; this issue will be discussed in the next section.

Integration on the *process level* is normally seen as the highest level, because it models business models independently of the infrastructure used.

5.5.2. Communication Paradigms and Middleware

Middleware has been mentioned above as a technology to link applications. Existing approaches differ strongly in their complexities and objectives, as discussed in Chapter 3 and section 5.2.3, where we briefly described *Inter-Process Communication* (*IPC*), *Remote Procedure Call* (*RPC*), *Event-Based Communication* (*EBC*), *Message-Oriented Middleware* (*MOM*), and *distributed object-oriented approaches.*

The XML-based approaches mentioned in different places in this book will be summarized below in preparation for the following sections. XML as an emerging *lingua franca* of the Internet is the basis not only for a "better Web/HTML" and the portable specification of semi-structured data, but also for new distributed application standards, particularly the *Simple Object Access Protocol* (*SOAP*), the *Web Service Description Language* (*WSDL*), and *Universal Description, Discovery, and Integration* (*UDDI*), to mention a few. SOAP handles messages and calls over different Internet protocols, e.g., HTTP, SMTP, etc. WSDL serves to describe interfaces and address Web services, and UDDI provides a sort of database to publish and search for Web services.

5.5.3. Distributed Cross-corporate Web Applications

The *distribution aspect* has gained increasing importance in the software-side implementation of Web applications. Just as links to remote Web pages are common today, distributed software will emerge from the meshed access to remote Web applications in the future. This can be interpreted as service-to-service communication, where the term *service* characterizes functionality offered over a well-defined interface. Web services have increasingly been implemented on the basis of XML. For example, eBay provides not only one single authentication system, but also supports Microsoft's Passport, and Google allows you to integrate their search function into external applications via SOAP. This "coarse-grained open component market" has dramatic consequences for system designers. The use of externally developed functionalities saves development costs, and the quality of components (services) may be better but this typically comes at the cost of losing "control" over these services. For example, security holes in Passport have dampened the initial enthusiasm, and the acceptance threshold for external services in security-critical applications is very high. On the other hand, a component-based approach can help to justify the money we spend for high-quality software products due to their high degree of reusability, and establish confidence in the quality of these components. Over the medium term, we therefore expect a market for Web Services, comparable to the wealth of services offered in our daily lives. Building on XML and basic technologies like SOAP, WSDL, and UDDI, other protocols are currently emerging, of which some are complementary and some are competing. These are protocols of the type necessary to handle business across the boundaries of a company. Figure 5-3 gives an overview of how these protocols depend on each other.

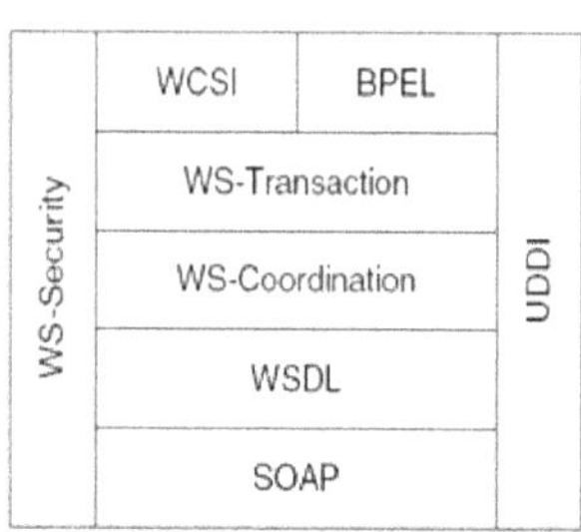

Figure 5.3: Protocol Stack for Web Services

The Web Services Transactions Specifications (*WS-Transaction*) describe an extensible framework to coordinate actions in distributed applications (*WS-Coordination*) and specific coordination types for atomic transactions and business transactions (IBM 2005a). *Atomic Transactions* allow you to coordinate short actions based on the 2-Phase-Commit protocol. This approach is suitable particularly to encapsulate proprietary formats of current transaction-oriented systems. *Business activities* in contrast are intended for long-lived actions, since they do not block resources over a lengthy period of time.

CHAPTER VI

TESTING WEB APPLICATIONS

Web applications have developed into an essential communication platform for many companies. Web applications are crucial for commerce, information exchange, and a host of social activities. For this reason Web applications have to offer high-performance, reliable, and easy-to-use services round the clock. Offering excellent Web applications for existing and future users represents a major challenge for quality assurance. Testing is one of the most important quality assurance measures. Traditional test methods and techniques concentrate largely on testing functional requirements. Unfortunately, they do not focus enough on the broad range of quality requirements, which are important for Web application users, such as performance, usability, reliability, and security. Furthermore, a major challenge of testing Web applications is the dominance of change. User requirements and expectations, platforms and configurations, business models, development and testing budgets are subject to frequent changes throughout the lifecycle of Web applications. It is, therefore, necessary to develop an effective scheme for testing that covers the broad range of quality characteristics of Web applications and handles the dominance of change, helping to implement and better understand a systematic, complete, and risk-aware testing approach. Such a test scheme forms the basis for building an exemplary method and tool box. Practical experience has shown that methodical and systematic testing founded on such a scheme is feasible and useful during the development and evolution of Web applications.

6.1. Introduction

Web applications pose new challenges to quality assurance and testing. Web applications consist of diverse software components possibly supplied by different manufacturers. The quality of a Web application is essentially determined by the quality of each software component involved and the quality of their interrelations. Testing is one of the most important instruments in the development of Web applications to achieve high-quality products that meet users' expectations.

Methodical and systematic testing of Web applications is an important measure, which should be given special emphasis within quality assurance. It is a measure aimed at finding errors and shortcomings in the software under test, while observing economic, temporal, and technical constraints. Many methods and techniques to test software systems are currently available. However, they cannot be directly applied to Web applications, which means that they have to be thought over and perhaps adapted and enhanced.

Testing Web applications goes beyond the testing of traditional software systems. Though similar requirements apply to the technical correctness of an application, the use of a Web application by heterogeneous user groups on a large number of platforms leads to special testing requirements. It is often hard to predict the future number of users for a Web application. Response times are among the decisive success factors in the Internet, and have to be tested early, despite the fact that the production-grade hardware is generally available only much later. Other important factors for the success of a Web application, e.g., usability, availability, browser compatibility, security, actuality, and efficiency, also have to be taken into account in early tests.

This chapter gives an overview of solutions, methods, and tools for Web application testing. The experiences from several research projects and a large number of industrial projects form the basis for the development of a structured test scheme for Web applications.

6.2. Fundamentals

6.2.1. Terminology

Testing is an activity conducted to evaluate the quality of a product and to improve it by identifying defects and problems. If we run a program with the intent to find errors, then we talk about *testing* (Myers 1979). Figure 6-1 shows that testing is part of analytical quality assurance measures (Bourque and Dupuis 2005). By discovering existing errors, the quality state of the program under test is determined, creating a basis for quality improvement, most simply by removing the errors found.

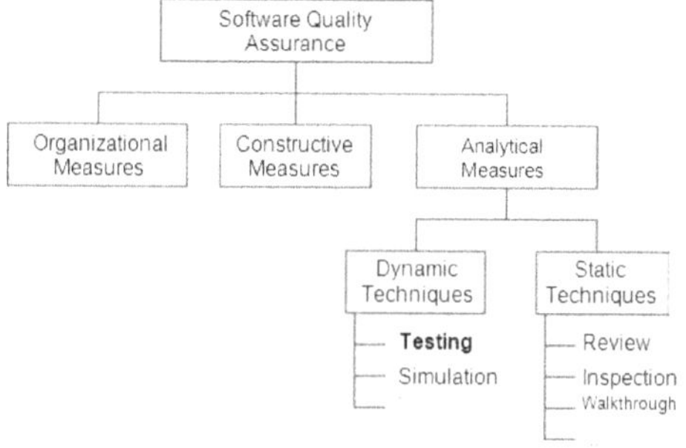

Figure 6.1: Structuring Software Quality Assurance

We say that an *error* is present if the actual result from a test run does not comply with the expected result. The expected result is specified, for example, in the requirements definition. This means that each deviation from the requirements definition is an error; more generally speaking, an error is "the difference between a computed, observed, or measured value or condition and the true, specified, or theoretically correct value or condition" (IEEE standard 610.12-1990).

This definition implies that the requirements definition used as a basis for testing is complete and available before implementation and test. A common phenomenon in the development of Web applications is that the requirements are often incomplete, fuzzy, and subject to frequent changes. Typically, there is an initial vision of the basic functionality. This vision is implemented for the initial release. As a result, the initial development lifecycle is followed by smaller cycles of functionality additions. Agile approaches (such as Extreme Programming, and (Highsmith 2002) for a general overview) focus on this iterative and evolutionary nature of the development lifecycle without an extensive written requirements definition. Consequently the goals, concerns, and expectations of the stakeholders have to form the basis for testing. This means that, for example, each deviation from the value typically expected by users is also considered an error.

Now, different stakeholders generally have different expectations, and some of these expectations may even be competing and fuzzy. For this reason, stakeholder expectations won't be a useful guideline to decide whether a result is erroneous unless agreement on a set of expectations has been reached and made available in testable form (see Chapter 2). To support the tester in gaining insight into the users' world and to better understand users' expectations, the tester should be involved as early as possible in the identification and definition of requirements.

When talking about a *test* in the further course of this chapter, we mean a set of test cases for a specific object under test (i.e., a Web application, components of a Web application, or a system that runs a Web application). A single *test case* describes a set of inputs, execution conditions, and expected results, which are used to test a specific aspect of the object under test (IEEE standard 610.12-1990).

6.2.2. *Quality Characteristics*

A user does not only expect an application to behave in a certain way; he or she also expects that certain functions are available 24 hours per day and 7 days a week (24x7). Moreover, users expect the application to be easy to use, reliable, fast, compatible with other systems and future versions, and the like. In addition to the behavior it is, therefore, important to test the application as to whether or not it meets its quality requirements, i.e., the kinds of quality characteristics expected by users.

Chapter 2 described the different quality characteristics in the context of Web applications. A general taxonomy for quality characteristics of software products is specified in the ISO/IEC 9126-1 standard. This standard mentions six principal categories of characteristics – functionality, reliability, usability, efficiency, maintainability, and portability – and breaks them down further into sub-characteristics.

Quality requirements play an essential role when testing Web applications. Though they are generally similar to quality requirements for traditional software systems, they often reach beyond them in both their breadth and depth (Offutt 2002). Due to the great significance of distinct quality characteristics and the differences as to how they can be tested, many methods for Web application testing concentrate on one or a few specific quality characteristics. However, all quality characteristics are important for the overall quality of a Web application. Testing has to ensure that they are successfully implemented.

6.2.3. Test Objectives

Testing won't lead to quality improvement unless errors are detected and removed. The main test objective is to find errors, rather than to show their absence. Software tests are unsuitable to prove the absence of errors. If a test doesn't find errors, then this does not mean that the tested application doesn't contain any. They may simply not have been detected yet.

The large number of quality characteristics to be considered, and all potential input values and input combinations, including all potential side conditions and processes, make it impossible to achieve complete test coverage. Even broad test coverage is typically impossible within the often extremely short development cycles. The inevitable consequences are flaws in tested functions and a higher risk of errors persisting undetected. These are the reasons why testing tends towards a risk-based approach. Those parts of an application where errors go undetected, and where these errors would have the most critical consequences, should be tested first and with the greatest effort. Exploring the sources of risk may point to defects more directly than basing tests mainly on requirements (Bach 1999). As a consequence, a further important test objective is to bring that risk to light, not simply to demonstrate conformance to stated requirements.

A test run is successful if errors are detected, respectively additional information about problems and the status of the application is acquired. Unsuccessful tests, i.e., tests that do not find errors, are "a waste of time" (Kaner et al. 1999). This is particularly true in Web application development, where testing is necessarily limited to a minimum due to restricted resources and the extreme time pressure under which Web applications are developed. This situation also requires that serious errors should be discovered as early as possible to avoid unnecessary investments as the cost of finding and removing errors increases dramatically with each development phase (Kaner et al. 1999). Errors that happened in early development phases are hard to localize in later phases, and their removal normally causes extensive changes and the need to deal with consequential errors. Therefore we have to start testing as early as possible at the beginning of a project.

In addition, short time-to-market cycles lead to situations where "time has to be made up for" in the test phase to compensate for delays incurred in the course of the project. Testing effectiveness and the efficiency of tests are extremely important. In summary, we can say that testing in general, and for Web projects in particular, has to detect as many errors as possible, ideally as many serious errors as possible, at the lowest cost possible, within as short a period of time as possible, and as early as possible.

6.2.4. *Test Levels*

According to the distinct development phases in which we can produce testable results, we identify *test levels* to facilitate testing of these results.

- *Unit tests*: test the smallest testable units (classes, Web pages, etc.), independently of one another. Unit testing is done by the developer during implementation.
- *Integration tests*: evaluate the interaction between distinct and separately tested units once they have been integrated. Integration tests are performed by a tester, a developer, or both jointly.
- *System tests*: test the complete, integrated system. System tests are typically performed by a specialized test team.
- *Acceptance tests*: evaluate the system in cooperation with or under the auspice of the client in an environment that comes closest to the production environment. Acceptance tests use real conditions and real data.
- *Beta tests*: let friendly users work with early versions of a product with the goal to provide early feedback. Beta tests are informal tests (without test plans and test cases) which rely on the number and creativity of potential users.

As development progresses, one proceeds from a verification against the technical specification (if available) – as in unit tests, integration tests and system tests – to a validation against user expectations – as in acceptance tests and beta tests.

An inherent risk when performing the test levels sequentially according to the project's phases is that errors due to misunderstood user expectations may be found only at a late stage, which makes their removal very costly. To minimize this risk, testing has to be an integrated part of the product construction which should encompass the whole development process. Hence, quality-assurance measures like reviews or prototyping are used even before running unit tests. A strongly iterative and evolutionary development process reduces this risk since smaller system parts are frequently tested on all test levels (including those with validation against user expectations), so that errors can be found before they can have an impact on other parts of the system. This means that the sequence of test levels described above does not always dictate the temporal sequence for Web project testing but may be performed several times, e.g. once for each incrementation of functionality.

6.2.5. Role of the Tester

The intention to find as many errors as possible requires testers to have a "destructive" attitude towards testing. In contrast, such an attitude is normally difficult for a developer to have towards his or her own piece of software, the more so as he or she normally doesn't have sufficient distance to his or her own work after the "constructive" development and problem solving activity. The same perspective often makes developers inclined to the same faults and misunderstandings during testing that have led to errors during the implementation in the first place. For this reason, (Myers 1979) suggests that developers shouldn't test their own products.

In Web projects, we have an increased focus on unit tests which are naturally written by the developers. While this is a violation of Myers' suggestion, additional tests are typically performed by someone different from the original developer (e.g. by functional testers recruited from the client's business departments).

Since quality is always a team issue, a strict separation of testing and development is not advisable and has an inherent risk to hinder the close cooperation between developers and testers. After all, the objective pursued to detect errors is that errors will be removed by the developers. To this end, a clearly regulated, positive communication basis and mutual understanding are prerequisites. This means for the tester: "The best tester isn't the one who finds the most bugs or who embarrasses the most programmers. The best tester is the one who gets the most bugs fixed." (Kaner et al. 1999).

Since Web project teams are normally multidisciplinary, and the team cooperation is usually of short duration, it can be difficult for team members to establish the necessary trust for close collaboration between developers and testers.

6.3.   Test Specifics in Web Engineering

The basics explained in the previous section apply both to conventional software testing and Web application testing. What makes Web application testing different from conventional software testing?

The following points outline the most important specifics and challenges in Web application testing based on the application's characteristics (see section 1.3).

- Errors in the "content" can often be found only by costly manual or organizational measures, e.g., by proofreading. Simple forms of automated checks (e.g., by a spell checker) are a valuable aid but are restricted to a limited range of potential defects. Meta-information about the content's structuring and semantics or a reference system that supplies comparative values are often a prerequisite to be able to perform in-depth tests. If these prerequisites are not available, other approaches have to be found. For example, if frequently changing data about the snow situation in a tourist information system cannot be tested by accurate meta-information or comparative values, then the validity of the data can be heuristically restricted to two days to ensure the data's actuality.

- When testing the hypertext structure, we have to ensure that the pages are linked correctly, e.g., each page should be accessible via a link and, in turn, it should have a link back to the hypertext structure. In addition, all links have to point to existing pages, i.e., they mustn't be broken. *Broken links* represent frequent errors when statically pre-defined links become invalid, for example, when an external Web page is referenced, which has been removed or changed its structure. Another source of errors is the navigation via Web browser functions, e.g., "Back in History", in combination with the states in which a Web application can be. A typical example: If a user places an article in the virtual shopping cart while shopping online, then this article will remain in the shopping cart even if the user goes one step back in the browser history, displaying the previous page without that article.

- The soft, subjective requirements on the presentation level of Web applications, e.g., "aesthetics", are difficult to specify. However, this is an essential prerequisite for the tester to be able to clearly and objectively distinguish acceptable (and desired) behavior from faulty behavior. Moreover, only a few conventional methods and techniques for software testing are suitable for presentation testing. To test a presentation, methods from other disciplines, e.g., print publishing, and organizational measures have to be used, similarly to content quality assurance.

- The large number of potential devices and their different performance characteristics (*multi-platform delivery*) represent another challenge. Even if a tester had all potential devices at disposal, he or she would have to run test cases for each device. Though simulators for devices can be helpful since the tester doesn't have to physically provide for the devices, they are often faulty themselves, or they are unable to exactly map a device's properties, or they become available only after the introduction of a device.

- Due to the global availability and usage of Web applications, there are many challenges with regard to multilinguality and usability in Web application testing. The major challenge is to recognize cultural interdependencies and consider them adequately in the test. For example, reading orders in different cultures (e.g., Arabic, Chinese) imply specific lateral navigation aids in the browser window. Another difficulty stems from different lengths of text messages in different languages which may result in layout difficulties.

- The common "juvenility" and "multidisciplinarity" of teams are often tied to poor acceptance of methodologies and poor readiness to do testing. Often knowledge about methods, technologies, and tools has to be acquired in the course of a project. Different points of view with regard to testing have to be consolidated. Only a team of sensitive and experienced members will come to a good decision about the amount of testing – too much testing can be just as counterproductive as too little. Testers are often tempted to test everything completely, especially at the beginning.

- Web applications consist of a number of different software components (e.g., Web servers, databases, middleware) and integrated systems (e.g., ERP systems, content management systems), which are frequently supplied by different vendors, and implemented with different technologies. These components form the technical infrastructure of the Web application. The quality of a Web application is essentially determined by the quality of all the single software components and the quality of the interfaces between them. This means that, in addition to the components developed in a project, we will have to test software components provided by third parties, and the integration and configuration of these components. Many errors in Web applications result from the "immaturity" of single software components, "incompatibility" between software components, or faulty configuration of correct software components. (Sneed 2004) reports on an industrial project where the test strategy was to test the compatibility of the Web application with the technical environment in addition to testing the functionality of the Web application.

- The "immaturity" of many test methods and tools represents additional challenges for the tester. If a Web application is implemented with a new technology, then there are often no suitable test methods and tools yet. Or if initial test tools become available, most of them are immature, faulty, and difficult to use.

- The "dominance of change" makes Web application testing more complex than conventional software testing. User requirements and expectations, platforms, operating systems, Internet technologies and configurations, business models and customer expectations, development and testing budgets are subject to frequent changes throughout the lifecycle of a Web application. Adapting to new or changed requirements is difficult because existing functionality must be retested whenever a change is made. This means that one single piece of functionality has to be tested many times, speaking heavily in favor of automated and repeatable tests. This places particular emphasis on regression tests, which verify that everything that has worked still works after a change. Upgrades and migrations of Web applications caused by ever-changing platforms, operating systems or hardware should first run and prove successful in the test environment to ensure that there will be no unexpected problems in the production environment. A second attempt and an ordered relapse should be prepared and included in the migration plan – and all of this in the small time window that remains for system maintenance, in addition to 24x7 operation ("availability").

6.4.   Test Approaches

Agile approaches (such as Extreme Programming, and (Highsmith 2002) for a general overview) have increasingly been used in Web projects. While agile approaches focus on collaboration, conventional approaches focus on planning and project management. Depending on the characteristics of a Web project, it may be necessary to perform test activities from agile and conventional approaches during the course of the project. (Boehm and Turner 2003) describe at length how to find the right balance between agility and discipline on projects. This section will not introduce one specific approach for Web application testing. Instead, we will explain the characteristics of conventional and agile testing approaches, and show how they differ.

6.4.1. *Conventional Approaches*

From the perspective of a conventional approach, testing activities in a project include planning, preparing, performing, and reporting:

- *Planning*: The planning step defines the quality goals, the general testing strategy, the test plans for all test levels, the metrics and measuring methods, and the test environment.

- *Preparing*: This step involves selecting the testing techniques and tools and specifying the test cases (including the test data).

- *Performing*: This step prepares the test infrastructure, runs the test cases, and then documents and evaluates the results.

- *Reporting*: This final step summarizes the test results and produces the test reports.

On the one hand, conventional approaches define work results (e.g., quality plan, test strategy, test plans, test cases, test measurements, test environment, test reports) and roles (e.g., test manager, test consultant, test specialist, tool specialist) as well as detailed steps to create the work results (e.g., analyze available test data or prepare/supply test data). Agile approaches, on the other hand, define the quality goal and then rely on the team to self-organize to create software that meets (or exceeds) the quality goal.

Due to the short time-to-market cycles under which Web applications are developed, it is typical to select only the most important work results, to pool roles, and to remove unnecessary work steps. It is also often the case that "time has to be made up for" in the test phase to compensate for delays incurred in the course of the project. Therefore, test activities should be started as early as possible to shorten the critical path – the sequence of activities determining the project duration (IEEE standard 1490 – 1998) – to delivery. For example, planning and design activities can be completed before development begins, and work results can be verified statically as soon as they become available. Figure 6-2 shows that this helps shorten the time to delivery, which complies nicely with the short development cycles of Web applications.

6.4.2. *Agile Approaches*

Agile approaches assume that a team will find solutions to problems jointly and autonomously (reliance on self-organization). This also applies to testing. Therefore, testing is not a matter of roles but of close collaboration and best usage of the capabilities available in the team. This means that testing is an integrated development activity.

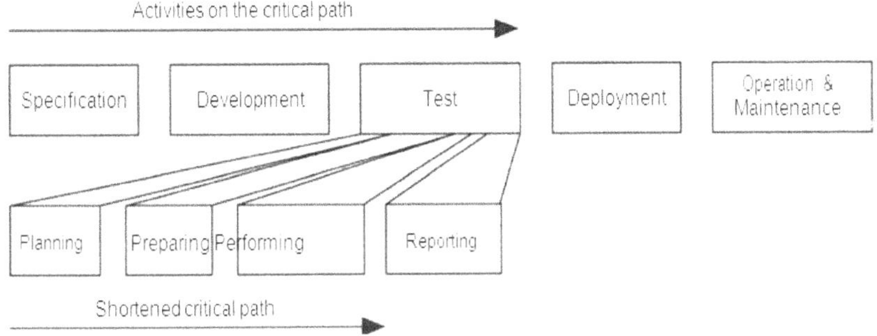

Figure 6.2: Critical Path of Activities

The entire team is jointly responsible for the quality and thus for testing.

Agile approaches omit activities that don't seem to promise an immediate benefit. For example, they hardly document things or write test plans; instead, they communicate directly, clearly express expectations and jointly commit to meeting them. Team members have to cooperate closely and "understand" each other to ensure that errors are detected and analyzed quickly, and removed efficiently.

In an agile approach, the developers perform unit tests, i.e. they test their own work. By automating these unit tests, they can be used as small "change detectors". Whenever a small piece of functionality no longer works as previously, the change will be detected immediately. The delay between introduction of an error and detection is reduced significantly which typically makes it easier for developers to correct the error since recent activities or changes are still fresh in their minds. In addition to quick feedback, automated tests are an important prerequisite for short development cycles and for *refactoring* (redesigning a program while keeping the semantics to reduce redundancies and increase the design quality; see Fowler et al. 1999).

There may be a dedicated tester on the team who supports the developers and assumes the quality-assurance leadership within the team. Also, the tester may prepare functional tests (which are on a higher abstraction level than the developers' unit tests) and make test scripts tolerant to changes. In addition, the tester may support the customer with writing functional tests.

The following practices of Extreme Programming (XP) have a particular influence on testing and quality assurance.

- *Pair programming*: accelerates the exchange of knowledge between developers, between developers and testers, and generally within the team. Similar to software inspections, it also helps to detect errors early.
- *An on-site customer*: is available for questions with regard to the requirements at any time, and takes decisions in this respect. Together with the tester, the on-site customer prepares functional tests, which can also be used for acceptance tests later on.
- *Continuous integration*: ensures that small steps help minimize the risk of changes, and walks through all tests to continuously verify that the entire system is faultless.
- *Test-first development*: means that tests are written before the code, ensuring that the "developer pair" thinks about the "what" before it implements the "how". These tests are automated, so that they can be used for continuous integration.

It may be interesting to note that Feature-Driven Development (another agile approach, see Palmer and Felsing 2002), does not use Pair programming but rather promotes code reviews. Both approaches, however, guarantee that static quality assurance techniques are applied to the code right from the start.

The agile approach described here refers mainly to unit and acceptance tests. In contrast, conventional approaches are used for integration and system tests ("testing in the large"; see Ambler 1999).

6.5. Test Scheme

This section describes a generic scheme for Web application testing. The scheme merges the testing basics – test cases, quality characteristics, and test levels – described above into a uniform and manageable setting. The scheme represents a model for Web application testing designed to better understand how testing can be organized and to support a systematic, comprehensive, and risk-aware testing approach. In the form introduced here, the scheme can be used to visualize the aspects involved in testing, structure all tests, and serve as a communication vehicle for the team.

6.5.1. *Three Test Dimensions*

Every test has a defined goal, e.g., to check the correctness of an algorithm, to reveal security violations in a transaction, or to find style incompatibilities in a graphical representation. The goals are described by the required quality characteristics on the one hand – e.g., correctness, security, compatibility – and by the test objects on the other hand – e.g., algorithms, transactions, representations. Thus, quality characteristics and test objects are mutually orthogonal. They can be seen on two separate dimensions whereby the first dimension focuses on quality characteristics relevant for the system under test, and the second and orthogonal way to view testing is to focus on the features of the system under test. This viewpoint implies that the test objects are executed and analyzed during test runs, while the quality characteristics determine the objectives of the tests. Both dimensions are needed to specify a test and can be used to organize a set of related tests.

For a systematic testing approach it is useful to distinguish between these two dimensions so it will be possible to identify all the test objects affecting a certain quality characteristic or, vice versa, all the quality characteristics affecting a certain test object. This is important since not all quality characteristics are equally – or at all – relevant for all test objects. For example, a user of an online shop should be free to look around and browse through the product offer, without being bothered by security precautions such as authentication or encryption, unless the user is going to purchase an item. Hence, while the quality characteristic "security" plays a subordinate role for the browsing functionality of the shop, it is of major importance for payment transactions. Distinguishing between these two dimensions allows us to include the relevance of different quality characteristics for each single test object.

In addition, a third dimension specifies when or in what phase of the software lifecycle a combination of test object and quality characteristic should be tested. This dimension is necessary to describe the timeframe within which the testing activities take place: from early phases such as requirements definition over design, implementation, and installation to operation and maintenance. As a result, testing can profit from valuable synergies when taking the activities over the whole lifecycle into account, e.g., by designing system tests that can be reused for regression testing or system monitoring. Furthermore, the time dimension helps to establish a general view of testing over all phases and allows a better understanding of what effects quality characteristics and test objects over time. It makes it easier to justify investments in testing in early phases since the possible payoff in later phases becomes clear.

If we join these three dimensions – *quality characteristics, test objects,* and *phases* – the result can be visualized as a three-dimensional cube as shown in Figure 6-3 (see Ramler et al. 2002). The cube contains all tests as nodes at the intersection of a specific quality characteristic, test object, and phase. The figure shows a possible structuring for the three dimensions, as suggested for Web application testing in the next section.

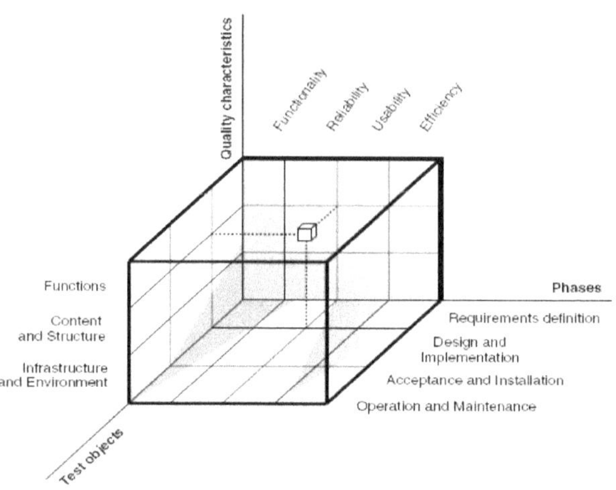

Figure 6.3: Test Scheme for Web Applications (Ramler et al. 2002)

6.5.2. Applying the Scheme to Web Applications

This section describes how the dimensions of the generic scheme introduced in the previous section can be structured to accommodate the special characteristics of Web applications and Web projects. In practice the structuring depends on the requirements of the system under test. Therefore, it is necessary to customize and detail the generic scheme according to the specific situation of the project.

Quality Characteristics

The *quality characteristics* dimension is determined by the quality characteristics that are relevant for the Web application under test. Thus, the quality characteristics relevant for testing originate in the objectives and expectations of the stakeholders and should have been described as non-functional requirements in the requirements definition (see Chapter 2). Additional information from other quality assurance measures and testing experience (e.g., typical risk factors, common exploits) should be considered when defining the quality characteristics dimension for a specific Web application.

For a generic classification we suggest to use the quality characteristics proposed by the ISO/IEC 9126-1 standard, respectively a representative subset such as *functionality, reliability, usability*, and *efficiency* (Olsina et al. 2001). A further breakdown results from the hierarchy of characteristics and sub-characteristics specified in the standard.

Test Objects

Traditional software testing describes the *test objects* dimension mainly by the functions of the system under test, specified in the form of functional requirements. The software testing literature (e.g. Myers 1979, Beizer 1990, Jorgensen 2002) elaborates on the design of test cases based on functional requirements at great length.

In contrast to conventional software systems, which focus mainly on functional requirements, Web applications also provide content, which frequently has to be developed and tested as part of a Web project (Powell et al. 1998). In document-centric Web applications, the content is often as important for their users as the actual functionality. For testing, this translates into the requirement to detect errors in the content including the hypertext structure and the presentation.

Whether or not a Web application meets users' expectations under real-world conditions depends also on the infrastructure and the environment of that Web application. This includes, for example, Web server configuration, network connection, integrated partner companies, and associated workflows. Users are confronted with the entire system. From the users' perspective, it doesn't really matter whether a Web application falls short of meeting their expectations due to a programming error or due to faulty Web server configuration. For this reason, it is necessary to extend testing to the infrastructure and the environment of a Web application. The generic test objects dimension should, therefore, include the *content and structure* and the *infrastructure and environment* of a Web application, in addition to *functions*.

Phases

The third dimension of the scheme – *phases* – focuses on the temporal sequence of Web application testing. This dimension shows when which test should be run within a Web application's lifecycle. This third dimension is structured according to a general development process or software lifecycle. The phases of a development process can differ from one Web project to another, depending on the selected process model . As a general rule, it is sufficient for a simple generic categorization to roughly distinguish between the following phases: *requirements definition, design and implementation, acceptance and installation*, and *operation and maintenance*.

The inclusion of all phases of the entire lifecycle makes clear that testing of a Web application doesn't end when a project is completed. For example, monitoring repeats a part of the tests regularly in normal operation to find new or existing errors after changes have been made to the infrastructure or to the environment. Typical examples for such changes are Web server updates or new Web browser versions. For instance, we have to periodically run compatibility tests to assure that users can access a Web application with any Web browser as soon as a new version becomes available, although no changes were made to the Web application itself.

6.5.3. *Examples of Using the Test Scheme*

To handle the three dimensions of the cube presented in the previous section, we use two-dimensional matrices representing slices or projections to remove one of the three dimensions. An example is Table 6-1, which shows the two dimensions test objects and quality characteristics. Thereby the scheme is used as an overview and conceptual framework to systematically arrange the methods and techniques applicable for Web application testing. The matrix can be used to establish a project-specific or company-wide method and tool box for Web application testing.

A further example is presented in (Ramler et al. 2002) which shows the application of the scheme in risk-based test management to prioritize tests for a Web application. The testing priorities have been defined in a joint workshop with testers, developers, users, and domain experts based on the priorities of the use cases (test objects) and non-functional requirements (quality characteristics). This approach facilitates test planning and test effort estimation and allows to trace back the priorities of each test to the priorities of the requirements.

6.6. Test Methods and Techniques

When testing Web applications, we can basically apply all methods and techniques commonly used in traditional software testing (see Myers 1979, Beizer 1990, Kaner et al. 1999, Jorgensen 2002). To take the specifics of Web applications into account, some of these test methods and techniques will have to be thought over, or adapted and expanded (e.g., "What influence factors have to be taken into account when testing compatibility with different Web browsers?"). In addition, we will most likely need new test methods and techniques to cover all those characteristics that have no correspondence in traditional software testing (e.g., testing of the hypertext structure).

The summary shown in Table 6-1 corresponds to the test scheme introduced in section 6.5 and is structured by the *test objects* dimension and the *quality characteristics* dimension. The table (see also Ramler et al. 2002) gives an exemplary overview of the methods, techniques, and tool classes for Web application testing described in the literature (e.g., Ash 2003, Dustin et al. 2002, Nguyen et al. 2003, Pressman 2005, Splaine and Jaskiel 2001). It shows typical representatives of test methods and techniques as a basis for arranging a corporate or project-specific method and tool box.

		Functions	Content and Structure	Infrastructure and Environment
Functionality	Suitability	Reviews and inspections, Test-driven development	Checklists, Lexical testing, Style guides, Reviews	
	Accuracy	Capture/Replay, Test-driven development	Static analysis, Link testing, Lexical testing, Reviews	Static analysis, Link testing
	Interopera-bility	Component Testing Cross-browser and cross-platform compatibility testing	Checklists, Test printing, Checklists, Reviews, Compatibility testing	Cross-browser and Cross-browser and cross-platform compatibility testing
	Compliance	Style guides, Test-driven development	Compatibility testing, Style guides, Reviews	cross-platform compatibility testing
	Security	Analysis of common attacks, Reviews and inspections		Analysis of common attacks, Forced-error testing, Ethical hacking
Reliability	Maturity Fault Tolerance	Endurance testing Forced-error testing, Stress testing		Endurance testing Forced-error testing, Low-resource testing, Stress testing
	Recoverability	Forced-error testing, Fail-over testing		Fail-over testing, Forced-error testing, Low-resource testing
Usability	Understanda-bility	Usability studies, Heuristic evaluation	Static readability analysis, Usability studies	
	Learnability	Usability studies, Usability studies, Heuristic evaluation		
	Operability Attractiveness	Heuristic evaluation	Publicity testing	Heuristic evaluation
Efficiency	Timing Behavior	Load and Stress testing, Monitoring		Load and Stress testing, Monitoring
	Resource Utilization	Endurance testing	Load testing	Endurance testing, Monitoring

The following subsections briefly describe typical methods and techniques for Web application testing.

6.6.1. *Link Testing*

Links within a hypertext navigation structure that point to a non-existing node (pages, images, etc.) or anchor are called *broken links* and represent well-known and frequently occurring errors in Web applications. To test for correct linking of pages (*link checking*), all links are systematically followed beginning on a start page, and then grouped in a link graph (*site map*). When running a link checking routine, one usually finds not only links that point to non-existing pages, but also pages which are not interlinked with others or so-called orphan pages. An *orphan page* can be reached via a link, but doesn't have a link back to the hypertext structure. To casual users it is not obvious where to go next, so they abandon the website. Pages are ideally designed so that they end with a suggestion of where the reader might go next.

In addition, when traversing links, one can often find additional data that supply indications to potential errors, e.g., the depth and breadth of the navigation structure, the distance between two related pages, measured by the number of links, or the load times of pages.

6.6.2. *Browser Testing*

A large number of different Web browsers can be used as the client for Web applications. Depending on the manufacturer (e.g., Microsoft, Mozilla, Netscape, Opera), or the version (e.g., Internet Explorer 5.0, 5.01, 5.5, 6.0), or the operating system (e.g., Internet Explorer for Windows XP/2000, Windows 98/ME/NT, or Macintosh), or the hardware equipment (e.g., screen resolution and color depth), or the configuration (e.g., activation of cookies, script languages, stylesheets), each Web browser shows a different behavior. Standards like the ones specified by W3C are often not fully implemented and "enhanced" by incompatible vendor-specific expansions. Web browser statistics and settings are available online (e.g., at http://www.webreference.com/stats/browser.html).

Browser testing tries to discover errors in Web applications caused by incompatibilities between different Web browsers. To this end, one normally defines a Web application's core functions, designs suitable test cases, and runs the tests on different target systems with different browser versions. During these tests, one should ask the following questions:

- Is the Web application's state managed correctly, or could inconsistent states occur when navigating directly to a page, for example, by using the browser's "Back" button?
- Can a (dynamically generated) Web page be bookmarked during a transaction, and can users navigate to that page later without having to enter a user name and password to log in?

- Can users use the Web application to open it in several browser windows (one or several instances of the Web browser) concurrently?
- How does the Web application react when the browser has cookies or script languages deactivated?

To limit the number of possible combinations of browsers, platforms, settings, and various other influence factors to a manageable set of test cases, the configurations of existing or potential users need to be analyzed, e.g., by evaluating log files and consulting browser statistics, to find popular combinations.

6.6.3. *Usability Testing*

Usability testing evaluates the ease-of-use issues of different Web designs, overall layout, and navigations of a Web application by a set of representative users. The focus is on the appearance and usability. A formal usability test is usually conducted in a laboratory setting, using workrooms fitted with one-way glass, video cameras, and a recording station. Both quantitative and qualitative data are gathered.

The second type of usability evaluation is a heuristic review. A heuristic review involves one or more human-interface specialists applying a set of guidelines to gauge the solution's usability, pinpoint areas for remediation, and provide recommendations for design change. This systematic evaluation employs usability principles that should be followed by all user interface designers such as error prevention, provision of feedback and consistency, etc.

In the context of usability testing the issue of making the Web accessible for users with disabilities has to be treated. Accessibility means that people with disabilities (e.g., visual, auditory, or cognitive) can perceive, understand, navigate, and interact with the Web. The Web Accessibility Initiative (WAI) of the W3C has developed approaches for evaluating Web sites for accessibility, which are also relevant for testing Web applications. In addition to evaluation guidelines the W3C provides a validation service (http://validator.w3.org/) to be used in combination with manual and user testing of accessibility features.

6.6.4. *Load, Stress, and Continuous Testing*

Load tests, stress tests, and continuous testing are based on similar procedures. Several requests are sent to the Web application under test concurrently by simulated users to measure response times and throughput. The requests used in these tests are generated by one or several "load generators". A control application distributes the test scripts across the load generators; it also synchronizes the test run, and collects the test results.

However, load tests, stress tests, and continuous testing have different test objectives:

- A *load test* verifies whether or not the system meets the required response times and the required throughput. To this end, we first determine load profiles (what access types, how many visits per day, at what peak times, how many visits per session, how many transactions per session, etc.) and the transaction mix (which functions shall be executed with which percentage). Next, we determine the target values for response times and throughput (in normal operation and at peak times, for simple or complex accesses, with minimum, maximum, and average values). Subsequently, we run the tests, generating the workload with the transaction mix defined in the load profile, and measure the response times and the throughput. The results are evaluated, and potential bottlenecks are identified.

- A *stress test* verifies whether or not the system reacts in a controlled way in "stress situations". Stress situations are simulated by applying extreme conditions, such as unrealistic overload, or heavily fluctuating load. The test is aimed at finding out whether or not the system reaches the required response times and the required throughput under stress at any given time, and whether it responds appropriately by generating an error message (e.g., by rejecting all further requests as soon as a pre-defined "flooding threshold" is reached). The application should not crash under stress due to additional requests. Once a stress situation is over, the system should recover as fast as possible and reassume normal behavior.

- *Continuous testing* means that the system is exercised over a lengthy period of time to discover "insidious" errors. Problems in resource management such as unreleased database connections or "memory leaks" are a typical example. They occur when an operation allocates resources (e.g., main memory, file handles, or database connections) but doesn't release them when it ends. If we call the faulty operation in a "normal" test a few times, we won't detect the error. Only continuous testing can ensure that the operation is executed repeatedly over long periods of time to eventually reproduce the resource bottleneck caused by this error, e.g., running out of memory.

6.6.5. Testing Security

Probably the most critical criterion for a Web application is that of security. The need to regulate access to information, to verify user identities, and to encrypt confidential information is of paramount importance. Security testing is a wide field, and will be discussed in this section only briefly; it does not represent a testing technique in the literal sense. It concerns issues in relation to the quality characteristic "security":

- *Confidentiality*: Who may access which data? Who may modify and delete data?
- *Authorization*: How and where are access rights managed? Are data encrypted at all? How are data encrypted?
- *Authentication*: How do users or servers authenticate themselves?
- *Accountability*: How are accesses logged?
- *Integrity*: How is information protected from being changed during transmission?

When testing in the field of security, it is important to proceed according to a systematic test scheme (see section 7.5). All functions have to be tested with regard to the security quality characteristic, i.e., we have to test each function as to whether or not it meets each of the requirements listed above. Testing security mechanisms (e.g., encryption) for correctness only is not sufficient. Despite a correctly implemented encryption algorithm, a search function, for example, could display confidential data on the result page. This is an error that test runs should detect, too. Typically, security testing must not only find defects due to intended but incomplete or incorrect functionality but also due to additional yet unwanted behavior that may have unforeseen side-effects or even contains malicious code. Unwanted, additional behavior is often exposed by passing input data unexpectedly to an application, e.g., by circumventing client-side input validation (Offutt et al. 2004).

6.6.6. *Test-Driven Development*

Test-driven development (Beck 2002) emerged from the test-first approach used in Extreme Programming, but it does not necessarily dictate an agile project approach. This means that we can use this technique even in conventional projects.

As the name implies, test-driven development is driven by (automated) tests, which are created prior to coding work. New code is written if a previously created test fails, i.e. developers have to write tests before they proceed to the implementation (refactoring). In that way, the design (and consequently the application) grows "organically" and every unit has its unit tests. The design naturally consists of many highly cohesive and loosely coupled components, facilitating the test.

Once the test fails, the developer implements what is absolutely necessary to successfully run the test as quickly as possible, even though this may mean violating a few principles. Once in a while, the developer eliminates the duplicate code introduced during the implementation. The many small unit tests can work as small "change detectors" during the course of the project.

Test-driven development has a beneficial psychological effect; the developer can concentrate on small steps and keep the larger goal ("clean code that works") in mind. This is opposed to the typical vicious circle; if increased pressure has left less time for testing, so that fewer things are tested, then more uncertainties lead to more pressure. Test-driven development ensures that a developer under increased stress simply runs existing automated tests more often. This enables him or her to get direct feedback that things are still working, which reduces stress and error probability.

6.7. Test Automation

Testing of large systems greatly benefits from tools that implement and automate methods and techniques (see above). This holds true particularly for iterative and evolutionary development of Web applications where an organized use of tools can support tests that are repeated frequently within short development cycles and narrow timeframes. But even once development is completed, changes to the infrastructure and the environment of a Web application often require tests to be repeated.

6.7.1. *Benefits and Drawbacks of Automated Tests*

Automation can significantly increase the efficiency of testing and, furthermore, enables new types of tests that also increase the scope (e.g. different test objects and quality characteristics) and depth of testing (e.g. large amounts and combinations of input data). Test automation brings the following benefits to Web application testing (see also Fewster and Graham 1999):

- Running automated regression tests on new versions of a Web application allows to detect defects caused by side-effects to unchanged functionality. These regression tests help to protect existing functionality of frequently changing Web applications.
- Various test methods and techniques would be difficult or impossible to perform manually. For example, load and stress testing requires automation and corresponding tools to simulate a large number of concurrent users. In the same way it is virtually impossible to fully test all the links of a Web application's extensive, cyclic hypertext structure manually.
- Automation allows to run more tests in less time and, thus, to run the tests more often leading to greater confidence in the system under test. Therefore, automation is a prerequisite for test-driven development, as developers run the tests for every bit of code they implement to successively grow the application.

- Also, the ability to quickly rerun an automated set of tests can help to shorten test execution time and to reduce the time-to-market when the bottleneck is repeating existing tests.

However, despite the potential efficiency gain that automated tests may provide, expectations about test automation are often unrealistically high. Test automation does not improve the effectiveness of testing (i.e. the total number of defects detected). Automating a test does not make it any more effective than running the same test manually. Usually, manual tests find even more defects than automated tests since it is most likely to find a defect the first time a test is run. If a test has been passed once, it is unlikely that a new defect will be detected when the same test is run again, unless the tested code is affected by a change. Furthermore, if testing is poorly organized, with ineffective tests that have a low capability of finding defects, automating these tests does not provide any benefits. Rather, the automation of a chaotic testing process only results in more and faster chaos.

Test automation is a significant investment. Although tools provide convenient features to automate testing, there is still a considerable amount of effort involved in planning, preparing, performing, and reporting on automated tests. And there is still a considerable amount of overhead involved in running the tests, including the deployment of the tests, the verification of the results, the handling of false alarms, and the maintenance of the test execution infrastructure. Automated tests have to be maintained too, as tests become obsolete or break because of changes that concern the user interface, output formats, APIs or protocols. In addition, the total cost of ownership of test tools involves not only the license fees but also additional costs such as training or dealing with technical problems since test tools are typically large and complex products.

The costs usually exceed the potential savings from faster and cheaper (automated) test execution. Thus, while it is sometimes argued that test automation pays off due to the reduced test execution cycles, in Web application testing the main benefit of automation comes from the advantages listed above that lead to improved quality and shorter time-to-market cycles. Even if the costs incurred by test automation may be higher compared with manual testing, the resulting benefits in quality and time call for this investment.

Thus, a sensible investment strategy uses tools to enhance manual testing, but does not aim to replace manual testing with automated testing. Manual tests are best to explore new functionality, driven by creativity, understanding, experience, and the gut feelings of a human tester. Automated tests secure existing functionality, find side-effects and defects that have been re-introduced, and enhance the range and accuracy of manual tests. Therefore, not all testing has to be automated. Partial automation can be very useful and various test tools are available to support the different kinds of testing activities.

6.7.2. *Test Tools*

Commonly used test tools support the following tasks:

- *Test planning and management*: These tools facilitate the management of test cases and test data, the selection of suitable test cases, and the collection of test results and bug tracking.
- *Test case design*: Tools available to design test cases support the developer in deriving test cases from the requirements definition or in generating test data.
- *Static and dynamic analyses*: Tools available to analyze Web applications, e.g., HTML validators or link checkers, try to discover deviations from standards.
- *Automating test runs*: Tools can automate test runs by simulating or logging as well as capturing and replaying the behavior of components or users.
- *System monitoring*: Tools available to monitor systems support us in detecting errors, e.g., by capturing system properties, such as memory consumption or database access.
- *General tasks*: Tools like editors or report generators are helpful and mentioned here for the sake of completeness. A detailed discussion would go beyond the scope of this book.

6.7.3. *Selecting Test Tools*

The current trend in test tools for Web applications is closely coupled with the continual evolution of Web technologies and modern development processes. A large number of different tools are available today. Descriptions of specific tools are normally of short validity, so they are omitted from this chapter. When selecting suitable tools for Web application testing, we always need to research and re-evaluate things. The test scheme introduced in this chapter can support us in selecting tools and building a well-structured and complete tool box. A comprehensive catalog of criteria for test tool evaluation is described in (Dustin et al. 2002). In addition, various Web pages maintain a continually updated summary of tools for Web application testing (e.g., at http://www.softwareqatest.com/qatweb1.html).

CHAPTER VII

PLANNING

Project planning, remains a very necessary activity when WebApps are built. Everyone plans to some extent, but the scope of planning activities varies among people involved in a WebE project. A Web engineer manages day-to-day work-planning, monitoring, and controlling technical tasks. A team leader plans, monitors, and coordinates the combined work of a WebE team. Other stakeholders generally have little interest in the details of the planning activity, but are *very* interested in the outcome. We plan so that their expectations can be met.

Because most WebApp increments are delivered over a time span that rarely exceeds 6 weeks, it's reasonable to ask: "Do we really need to spend time planning a WebApp effort? Shouldn't we just let a WebApp evolve naturally, with little or no explicit planning and only indirect management?" More than a few Web developers would opt for this approach, but that doesn't make them right!

Taking an agile approach to the planning activity, you adapt the effort and time spent on planning to the complexity of the WebApp increment to be deployed. If the WebApp increment is simple (e.g., the con-tent is well defined and functions are straightforward), planning will take very little time. If, on the other hand, the increment is complex in terms of content, functionality, constraints, and performance, planning will re-quire greater effort and will encompass each of the actions and tasks discussed in this chapter. Regardless of the characteristics of the increment, you must plan.

7.1.   Understanding the Scope

WebApp *Scope* is defined by answering the following questions:

- **Context.** How does the WebApp fit into a business context, and what constraints are imposed as a result of the context?
- **Information objectives.** What customer-visible content objects are used and produced by the WebApp increment?
- **Functionality.** What functions are initiated by the end user or invoked internally by the WebApp to meet the requirements defined in usage scenarios?
- **Constraints and performance.** What technical and environmental constraints will impact the framework activities that follow? What special performance issues (including security and privacy issues) will require design and construction effort?

Because it is difficult, if not impossible, to develop a meaningful plan without understanding the scope of the WebApp increment, the information derived during the communication activity must be examined with care. If scope is vague at this stage (and it may be), you have a bit of work to do before planning can commence.

7.1.1. What Communication Work Products Are Relevant?

All communication work products are relevant to the planning activity. In some cases, the only information available may be your written notes (*always* take notes!) and a set of usage scenarios that provide a description of the content and functions for the WebApp increment. If you take a more formal approach to communication, the following work products may be available for the planning activity:

- Statement describing business motivation for the overall WebApp
- Statement of overall objective for the WebApp
- List of user categories
- List of informational goals for the WebApp increment to be planned
- List of applicative (functional) goals for the WebApp increment to be planne
- Description of the increment (the statement of scope)
- List of content objects for the increment
- List of functions for the increment
- Set of usage scenarios that describe how each user category will interact with the increment

Although it's wonderful when all this information is available, it's not necessarily suffi cient for the planning activity. The information developed during the communication activity may not be as complete as the WebE team would like. It's important to know what to do when this occurs.

7.1.2. What If Further Details Are Required to Understand the Increment?

Human beings tend to apply a divide-and-conquer strategy when they are confronted with a complex or vague problem. Stated simply, the problem is partitioned into smaller problems that are more understandable. Because the communication activity makes no attempt to fully define every aspect of the content and functions to be delivered by the WebApp,[1] an *elaboration* strategy can be used when further details are required to understand the scope of the WebApp increment in a more complete manner. Elaboration begins with the information that has been developed as part of the communication activity. It is applied in two major areas:

to the *content* that is to be delivered with the WebApp increment and to the *functions* that are invoked as part of all user scenarios for the increment.

The usage scenarios imply the existence of a number of major content objects and the functions that are related to them. However, these content objects and functions have *not* been explicitly identified during communication. You have three options: (1) proceed with planning and worry about the elaboration of content and functionality during the modeling activity, (2) do a bit of elaboration now, so that planning can be more reliable, or (3) do a complete elaboration to be sure you really understand this increment.

There is no "best" option here. The team may feel that technical work (in this case, analysis modeling) should begin (time is *always* of the essence) and may opt to develop the best plan they can with whatever information is now available. Alternatively, the team may choose to do a small amount of elaboration so that the plan can properly allocate technical work based on the content and functions that will be derived. Finally, the team may decide to do analysis modeling right now and completely elaborate before the plan is developed.

As an example, let's assume that the second option is chosen. The team will do a bit of elaboration now so that the plan can be completed but will delay the development of a more complete elaboration until the modeling activity commences.[2] Since the usage scenarios refer to a "space," the WebE team elaborates on the concept:

Space—a defined floor plan for a home or a small business

Content objects:

SpaceIdentifier
Name of space

Customer name

Walls
Wall name (displayed as a number)

Start and end coordinates

Doorways
Wall ID

Door size

Door start coordinate

Windows
Wall ID

Window size

Window start coordinate

... and so on for all content objects associated with this increment.

Functions (associated with "space"):

Specify and draw walls

Specify and draw doorways

Specify and draw windows

Compute size of each room

Save/retrieve a named space

Security protection is required

Update/delete a named space

Security protection is required

Print a named space

... and so on for all functions associated with this increment.

The amount of effort associated with this elaboration is relatively small, but the payoff can be significant. For example, you now know that the team will have to develop at least seven functions associated with the creation of a user space. The work associated with this is allocated as part of the planning activity.

7.1.3. What If Gaps Still Exist in Your Understanding?

You cannot expect to achieve comprehensive understanding at the planning stage. You'll have to accept the fact that things remain a bit uncertain, even after you've elaborated the information derived during the communication activity—it's one of the risks inherent in all engineering work. More important, you'll have to complete the planning activity with imperfect information and move on.

As you move further into the WebE process, your understanding will improve as modeling is conducted. However, it's reasonable to assume that there will be a few surprises (some may be nasty) as construction proceeds. The team will have to adapt and move forward.

7.2.   Refining Framework Activities

The WebE team must now choose the framework actions and tasks that are right for the remaining WebE work to be applied to the increment. The increment to be built:

- **Modeling.** Actions and tasks that lead to the creation of analysis and design models that assist the WebE team and other stakeholders to better understand the WebApp and how it is to be constructed.

- **Construction.** Actions and tasks required for code generation (either manual or automated) and testing

- **Deployment.** Actions and tasks that deliver the WebApp increment to the end users who evaluate it and provide feedback based on the evaluation.

These framework activities are applicable to all WebApp increments. The problem is to refine the set of actions and tasks that are appropriate for this increment

7.2.1. *What Actions and Tasks Are Required?*

WebE framework actions and tasks are refined by "melding" characteristics of the increment and the process. One way to accomplish this is to create a table similar to the one illustrated in Figure 7.1. The top row of the table lists the key content objects and functions to be delivered as part of the increment deployment. The first column lists the set of framework actions and tasks for modeling, construction, and deployment.

The WebE team selects the set of actions and tasks that are most appropriate for the WebApp increment to be engineered. Although some team members will argue in favor of a very sparse list, it is best to spend the time to develop a set of actions and tasks that will lead to a high-quality result. It's worth noting that just because a task is listed in the table it does not necessarily have to be used for every content object and function. The final decision is left to the Web engineer who will do the work. However, if the Web engineer decides to forego the WebE task, he or she must be able to justify the decision and is ultimately responsible for the quality of the work product produced.

Figure 7.1 illustrates only a portion of the table that would be created for the SafeHomeAssured.com WebApp. In the portion shown, the content and functions for the usage scenarios are illustrated.

Develop a layout of the space to be monitored.

Get recommendations for sensor layout for my space.

Content objects—**Walls, Doorways,** and **Windows**—are listed in the fi rst section of the top row. Functions (e.g., *Specify and draw walls*) are listed next.

After a brief discussion, the WebE team selects the set of tasks that will be used to model, construct, and deploy these content objects and functions. Refer-ring to the fi gure, you'll note that the team has adapted the generic framework, rearranging some tasks, modifying others, and adding a few. In every instance, process agility and the quality of the end result will guide decision making. The internal matrix within the table is used to indicate which actions and tasks are applicable to which content and functionality. Not every action and task will be applied to every content object and function.

It is important to note that the set of actions and tasks defined for one increment is *not* necessarily the same set that is used for the next increment. The size and complexity of the work associated with each increment guides the WebE team in the selection of the framework tasks that will be applied.

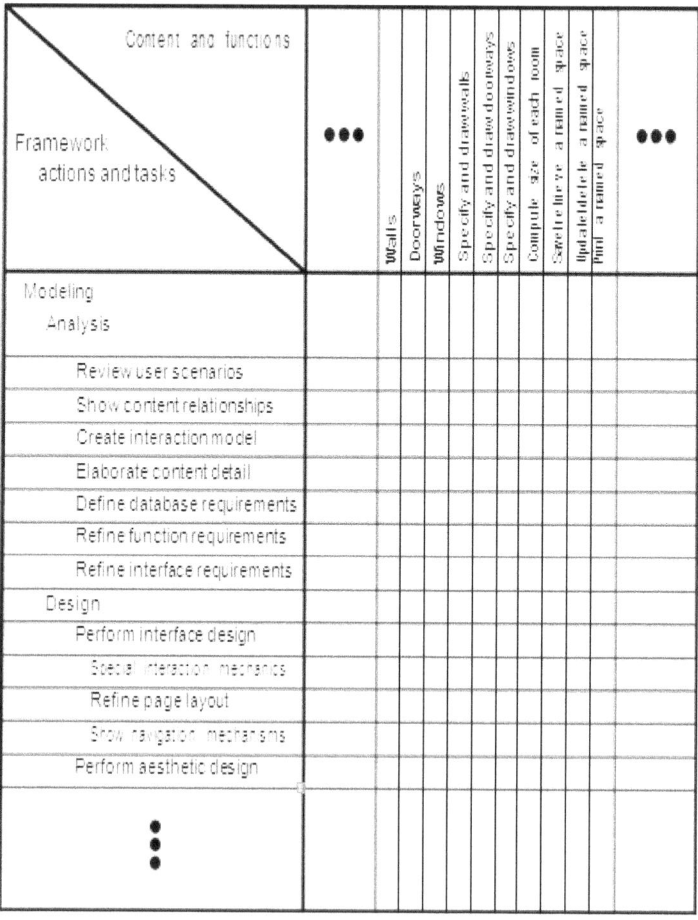

Figure 7.1: Melding the Problem and the Process

7.2.2. *What Work Products Will Be Produced?*

The number of intermediate work products (e.g., modeling representations, inter-face sketches, navigation maps) should be kept to the minimum that is necessary to provide appropriate guidance for the next framework action or task. Three criteria should guide the team:

- Is the work product absolutely necessary to better understand the WebApp increment and to achieve a high-quality result?
- Will the work product serve as a useful foundation for work to be conducted in subsequent WebE tasks?
- Does the work product provide information that can be used during the engineering of other WebApp increments?

If the answer to any of these questions is "yes," then you should consider creating the work product. Creating unnecessary work products not only wastes effort but can also calcify the WebApp and encourage developers to resist changes that might be very appropriate.

7.2.3. *What Is the Appropriate Way to Assess Quality?*

You can do it right, or you can do it over again. If a WebE team stresses quality in all framework activities, the team reduces the amount of rework that it must do. That results in lower costs and, more importantly, improved time-to-market.

But it's not enough to talk the talk by saying that quality is important. You have to explicitly define what you mean when you say "WebApp quality" and define a set of tasks that will help ensure that every work product exhibits high quality.

When we discuss WebApp quality in this book, we refer to completeness and accuracy of the problem definition, the commodity of the solution design, the firmness of construction, and the overall degree to which the WebApp increment meets the needs of all stakeholders .

In order to ensure the quality of work products as they are produced, the WebE team can conduct *pair walkthroughs.* This approach, adapted from the concept of *pair programming* in the *Extreme Programming* method [Bec99] [Jef01], suggests that all work products be reviewed by a pair of Web engineers. The producer of the work product presents it to another team member who looks for errors, inconsistencies, and omissions. Working together, the pair tries to improve the quality of the work product.

In cases where the work product is complex or its impact will be critical to the success of the project, the WebE team may schedule a *team walkthrough*—a review form that involves a number of team members and is guided by a distinct set of rules.

7.2.4. *How Should Change Be Managed?*

If you don't manage change, it manages you. And that's never good. It's very easy for a stream of uncontrolled changes to turn a well-run WebE project into chaos. For that reason, planning for change is an essential part of the planning activity.

Changes arise from a number of different sources: (1) nontechnical stakeholders may have an afterthought[5] about the WebApp in general or the increment that is currently being developed, (2) end users may request different modes of interaction or demand different functions or content, or (3) Web engineers may learn that unexpected modifications are required to achieve WebApp requirements.

In every case, the change that is requested must be described unambiguously, evaluated to determine the impact on the increment and the overall WebApp, and assessed to estimate the level of effort required to make the change. The problem is that all these change management activities take resources and time—things that are often in short supply as the WebE team is working on an increment. Yet, stakeholders want the changes to be made.

Later in this chapter we'll discuss change management—an umbrella activity that is designed to address the compelling need to make the changes that are requested, while at the same time lightening the immediate burden of change on a WebE team that is immersed in modeling, construction, and deployment.

7.3. Building a WebE Team

Web engineering emphasizes agility, and the agile philosophy stresses the importance of individual competency coupled with group collaboration. These are critical success factors for a WebE team. Cockburn and Highsmith [Coc01] note this when they write:

Interestingly, people working together with good communication and interaction can operate at noticeably higher levels than when they use their individual talents. We see this time and again in brainstorming and joint problem-solving sessions. Therefore, agile project teams [WebE teams] focus on increasing both individual competencies and collaboration levels. To make effective use of the competencies of each team member and to foster effective collaboration throughout a project, WebE teams should be *self-organizing.* In the context of Web engineering, *self*-organization implies three things:

1. The WebE team organizes itself for the work to be done
2. The team organizes the process framework to best accommodate its local environment,

3. The team organizes the work schedule to best achieve delivery of the WebApp increment.

Self-organization has a number of technical benefits, but more importantly, it serves to improve collaboration and boost team morale. In essence, the team serves as its own management. Ken Schwaber [Sch02] addresses these issues when he writes: "The team selects how much work it believes it can perform within the iteration [increment], and the team commits to the work. Nothing demotivates a team as much as someone else making commitments for it. Nothing motivates a team as much as accepting the responsibility for fulfilling commitments that it made itself."

7.3.1. How Do We Recognize a "Good" WebE Team?

The objective for every organization is to create a WebE team that exhibits cohesive-ness. In their book, Peopleware, DeMarco and Lister [Dem98] discuss this issue.

We tend to use the word team fairly loosely in the business world, calling any group of people assigned to work together a "team." But many of these groups just don't seem like teams. They don't have a common definition of success or any identifiable team spirit. What is missing is a phenomenon that we call *jell.*

A jelled team is a group of people so strongly knit that the whole is greater than the sum of the parts ...

Once a team begins to jell, the probability of success goes way up. The team can become unstoppable, a juggernaut for success . . . They don't need to be man-aged in the traditional way, and they certainly don't need to be motivated. They've got momentum.

DeMarco and Lister contend that members of jelled teams are significantly more productive and more motivated than average. They share a common goal, a common culture, and in many cases, a "sense of eliteness" that makes them unique.

7.3.2. Why Don't Teams Jell and What Can Be Done to Help?

Sadly, a WebE team can suffer from *team toxicity*—a malady defined by five factors that "foster a potentially toxic team environment" [Jac98].

- A frenzied work atmosphere in which team members waste energy and lose focus on the objectives of the work to be performed.
- High frustration caused by personal, business, or technological factors that causes friction among team members.

- "Fragmented or poorly coordinated procedures" or a poorly defined or improperly chosen process model that becomes a roadblock to accomplishment.
- Unclear definition of roles resulting in a lack of accountability and resultant Finger-pointing.
- "Continuous and repeated exposure to failure" that leads to a loss of confidence and a lowering of morale

In general, each of these toxins can be avoided if the WebE team is self-organizing. A self-organizing team has access to all information required to do the job, thereby avoiding a frenzied work environment in which people are scrambling to find vital information. A self-organizing team has control over the process that is employed, the work products that are produced, the work schedule that is defined, and the quality and change management activities that are implemented. Therefore, the team avoids the frustration that occurs when there is a lack of control. A self-organizing team establishes its own mechanisms for accountability (e.g., pair walkthroughs are a good way to accomplish this) and defines a series of corrective approaches when a member of the team fails to perform.

Every WebE team experiences small failures. The key to avoiding an atmosphere of failure is to establish team-based techniques for feedback and problem solving. In addition, failure by any member of the team must be viewed as a failure by the team itself. This leads to a team-oriented approach to corrective action, rather than the finger-pointing and mistrust that grows rapidly on toxic teams.

7.3.3. Can a WebE Team Manage Itself?

Some might argue that do-it-yourself team management is akin to do-it-yourself brain surgery, but we disagree (at least some of the time[6]). If a WebE team is experienced and competent, it is possible to develop WebApp increments without an official "project manager." A team leader should be appointed to coordinate communication and work tasks, but members of the team can assess progress and problems by conducting daily team meetings to coordinate and synchronize the work that must be accomplished for that day. These brief meetings (e.g., 15 to 20 minutes) address four key questions:

- What have we accomplished since the last meeting?
- What needs to be accomplished before the next meeting?
- How will each team member contribute to accomplishing what needs to be done?
- What roadblocks exist that have to be overcome?

As answers to each of these questions emerge, the team adapts its approach in a way that accomplishes the work to be performed. As each day passes, continual self-organization and collaboration move the team toward a completed WebApp increment.

If a WebApp project is very complex, a large team or multiple teams may be required. In such cases (or in the case where the members of a team are inexperienced) a project manager can serve a vitally important role.

7.3.4.   How Do We Build a Successful Team?

In his best-selling book on a computer industry long past, Tracy Kidder [Kid00] tells the story of a computer company's heroic attempt to build a computer to meet the challenge of a new product built by a larger competitor.[7] The story is a metaphor for teamwork, leadership, and the grinding stress that all technologists encounter when critical projects don't go as smoothly as planned.

A summary of Kidder's book hardly does it justice, but these key points [Pic01] have particular relevance as you work to build an effective WebE team:

- **A set of team guidelines should be established.** These encompass what is expected of each person, how problems are to be dealt with, and what mechanisms exist for improving the effectiveness of the team as the project proceeds.
- **Strong leadership is a must.** The team leader must lead by example and by contact and must exhibit a level of enthusiasm that gets other team members to "sign up" psychologically for the work that confronts them.
- **Respect for individual talents is critical.** Not everyone is good at everything. The best teams make use of individual strengths. The best team leaders allow individuals the freedom to run with a good idea.
- **Every member of the team should commit.** The main protagonist in Kidder's book calls this "signing up."
- **It's easy to get started, but it's very hard to sustain momentum.** The best teams never let an "insurmountable" problem stop them. Team members develop a "good enough" solution and proceed, hoping that the momentum of forward progress may lead to an even better solution later in the project.

Scott Rosenberg [Ros07] discusses the challenges that face software developers (and Web engineers) in a book with the intriguing title *Dreaming in Code.* He writes about an open source team working to develop a product called *Chandler* (chandler.osafoundation.org), innovative software for workgroup support. In discussing challenges that face technical teams, he writes:

It's rare for a group of software developers to work together on a series of projects over time; in this they are less like sports teams or military units or musical ensembles and more like the forces of pros who assemble to make a movie and then disperse and re-combine for the next film. So, while individual programmers and managers may carry with them a wealth of experience and knowledge of techniques that have served them well in the past, each time they begin a new project with a new team, they are likely to end up pressing the reset button and having to devise a working process from first principles.

We think Rosenberg has it half right. It is true that Web engineers and software developers in general are very much like a movie production company—each creative and knowledgeable in his area of specialty. But we don't think it's either necessary or desirable to "devise a working process from first principles" every time a new project is initiated. Successful teams can make use of a well-defined process framework without any reinvention. This saves them time, and, more importantly, it establishes a foundation from which a high-quality product can emerge.

7.3.5. *What Are the Characteristics of a Good Team Leader?*

In an excellent book on technical leadership, Jerry Weinberg [Wei86] suggests an MOI model of leadership:

- **Motivation.** The ability to encourage technical people to produce to their best ability. This can be accomplished by providing incentives for high performance and imposing consequences for poor performance.
- **Organization.** The ability to mold existing processes (or invent new ones) that will enable the initial concept to be translated into a final product.
- **Ideas or innovation.** The ability to encourage people to create and feel creative even when they must work within bounds established for a particular WebApp.

Weinberg suggests that successful project leaders apply a problem-solving   management style. That is, a leader of a WebE team should concentrate on understanding the problem to be solved, managing the flow of ideas, and at the same time, letting everyone on the team know (by words and, far more important, by actions) that quality counts and that it will not be compromised.

7.4. Managing Risk

Risk management encompasses a series of tasks that help a WebE team to under-stand and manage the many problems that can plague a WebApp project. A risk is a potential problem—it might happen, it might not. But, regardless of the outcome, it's a really good idea to identify it, assess its probability of occurrence, estimate its impact, and establish a contingency plan should the problem actually occur.

A WebE team considers risk at two different levels of granularity:

1. The impact of risk on the entire WebApp project.

2. The impact of risk on the successful deployment of the WebApp increment currently being engineered.

At the project level, many risk-related questions must be asked and answered: Can planned WebApp increments be delivered within the time frame defined? Will these increments provide ongoing value for end users while additional increments are being engineered? How will requests for change impact delivery schedules? Does the team understand the required Web engineering methods, technologies, and tools? Is the available technology appropriate for the job? Will likely changes require the introduction of new technology?

At the increment level, concerns are more basic. Has the communication activity developed sufficient information for modeling, construction, and deployment? Is the refined process framework appropriate for the increment to be developed? Does the team have the right mix of skills to build this increment? Are content and function adequately defined? Does the increment pose a technology challenge?

Risk management is initiated during the planning activity but is actually an umbrella activity that is revisited throughout the process flow. The challenge for a WebE team is to do enough of it to be proactive about risk, but not so much that it slows other development work to a crawl. Let's examine the basics.

7.4.1. How Do We Identify Risks?

At some point during the planning activity, the WebE team collectively addresses the fundamental question: "What can go wrong?" Each team member is asked to make a list of risks that can be organized into one of the following categories:

1. People risks.

2. Product risks.

3. Process risks.

People risks are potential problems that can be directly traced to some human action or failing. For example, it's likely that the WebApp increment will require components developed using XML, but the team currently has no one with XML experience. A technology-related people risk has been identified. Or maybe a specific stakeholder has been uncooperative in the past when information requests have been made, and yet, the required information is crucial to a successful outcome. A communication-related people risk has been identified.

Product risk can normally be traced to potential problems associated with WebApp content, functions, constraints, or performance. For example, a risk that could impact the tight delivery time for the first SafeHomeAssured.com increment (an informational WebApp) is discovered only after construction has commenced. A major content object (a comprehensive description of *SafeHome* products) is out-dated and may require substantial modification before it can be deployed. A performance risk associated with a later SafeHomeAssured.com increment (in-home video monitoring) might be questionable control and monitoring interfaces for video and audio equipment.

Process risks are problems that are tied to the framework actions and tasks that have been chosen by the team. In some cases, too much process can be a potential risk. For example, the team has decided to do a thorough analysis model and has specified actions and tasks (and related work products) to accomplish this. For the fourth increment of the SafeHomeAssured. com WebApp (implement a layout for the space to be secured and recommend sensors for that space), a process risk might be that the work associated with developing a complete analysis model may be too time consuming and will cause a delay in design and construction activities.

The lists of possible risks are collected from team members and consolidated by category. The WebE team then meets to evaluate them.

7.4.2.   How Do We Evaluate Risks?

Once a consolidated list of risks has been developed, the WebE team performs a quick evaluation. Each risk is briefly discussed and evaluated in two ways:

1.   The likelihood or probability that the risk will become a reality.
2.   The con-sequences of the problems associated with the risk, should it occur.

The intent is to consider risks in a manner that leads to prioritization. No WebE team has the time or the resources to address every possible risk with the same degree of rigor. By prioritizing risks, the team can allocate resources where they will have the most impact.

Once probability and impact have been estimated, the team can build a risk table .A sample risk table is illustrated in Figure 7.2. The three columns of the table reflect the risks, their probability (normally represented as a percentage), their impact on schedule and/or cost (often represented using an ordinal scale of 1 [low] to 4 [high]).

Once the columns of the risk table have been completed, the table is sorted by probability and then by impact. Alternatively, a composite score derived from *probability* 3 *impact* can be calculated and the table sorted on this basis. High-probability, high-impact risks percolate to the top of the table, and low-probability risks drop to the bottom. This accomplishes first-order risk prioritization. The team studies the resultant sorted risk table and defines a cutoff line. The *cutoff line* (drawn horizontally at some point in the table) implies that only risks that lie above.

7.4.3. *How Do We Develop Contingency Plans?*

Since the overall development time span for each WebApp increment is short, writ-ten contingency plans are *not* developed as part of the WebE process framework. But that doesn't mean that the WebE team simply ignores high-priority risks. The members of the team consider each risk that falls above the cutoff line in the risk table and answers three questions:

- How can we avoid the risk altogether?
- What factors can we monitor to determine whether the risk is becoming more or less likely?
- Should the risk become a reality, what are we going to do about it?

The answers to these questions can be recorded (as informal notes) by the team leader.

7.5. Developing a Schedule

Fred Brooks, the well-known author of *The Mythical Man-Month* [Bro95], was once asked how software projects fall behind schedule. His response was as simple as it was profound: "One day at a time."

The reality of any technical project (whether it involves building a hydroelectric plant or developing a WebApp) is that hundreds of small tasks must occur to accomplish a larger goal. Some of these tasks lie outside the mainstream and may be completed without worry about impact on the completion date. Other tasks lie on the "critical path." If these critical tasks fall behind schedule, the completion date for the WebApp increment is put into jeopardy.

The WebE team's objective is to list all WebE actions and tasks for an increment, build a network that depicts their interdependencies, identify the tasks that are critical within the network, and then track their progress to ensure that any delay will be recognized "one day at a time." To accomplish this, the team leader must have a schedule that has been defined at a degree of resolution that allows progress to be monitored and the project to be controlled.

WebApp project scheduling is an activity that allocates the estimated effort for specific WebE tasks across the planned time line (duration) for building an increment. It is important to note, however, that the overall WebApp schedule evolves over time. During the first iteration of the WebE process framework, a macroscopic schedule is developed. This type of schedule identifies all WebApp increments and projects the dates on which each will be deployed. As the development of the increments gets under way, the entry for the increment on the macroscopic schedule is refined into a detailed schedule. Here, specific WebE tasks (required to accomplish an activity) are identified and scheduled.

Scheduling for WebE projects can be viewed from two rather different perspectives. In the first, an end date for the release of a WebApp has already (and irrevocably) been established. The WebE organization is constrained to distribute effort within the prescribed time frame. The second view of WebApp scheduling assumes that rough chronological boundaries have been discussed but that the end date is set by the WebE organization. Effort is distributed to make best use of resources, and an end date is defined after careful analysis of the Web-App. Unfortunately, the first situation is encountered far more frequently than the second.

7.5.1. *What Is Macroscopic Scheduling?*

As an example of macroscopic scheduling, consider the SafeHomeAssured.com Web-App. There are, seven increments were identified for the project:

Increment 1: Basic company and product information

Increment 2: Detailed product information and downloads

Increment 3: Product quotes and processing product orders

Increment 4: Space layout and security system design

Increment 5: Information and ordering of monitoring services

Increment 6: Online control of monitoring equipment

Increment 7: Accessing account information.

Risks	Probability	Impact
People		
Little XML experience on team	80%	3
Stakeholders uncooperative	60%	2
Senior manager may change midstream	40%	1
Product		
Informational content may be outdated	50%	2
Algorithms may not be adequately defined	80%	3
Security for WebApp more difficult than expected	80%	3
Database integration more difficult than expected	40%	3
Space def. capability more difficult than expected	70%	3
Process		
Not enough emphasis on communication	60%	2
Too many analysis tasks (too much time spent)	30%	1
Not enough emphasis on navigation design	40%	2
⋮	⋮	⋮

Figure 7.2: Sample Risk Table Prior to Sorting

The WebE team consults and negotiates with stakeholders and develops a *preliminary* deployment schedule for all seven increments. A time line for this schedule is illustrated in Figure 7.3.

It is important to note that the deployment dates (represented by diamonds on the time line) are preliminary and may change as more detailed scheduling of the increments occurs. However, this macroscopic schedule provides management with an indication of when content and functionality will be available and when the entire project will be completed. As a preliminary estimate, the team will work to deploy all increments with a 12-week time line. It's also worth noting that some of the increments will be developed in parallel (e.g., increments 3, 4, and 7). This assumes that the team will have sufficient people to do this parallel work.

7.5.2. *What Is Increment Scheduling?*

Once the macroscopic schedule has been developed, the team is ready to schedule work tasks for a specific increment. To accomplish this, you can use a generic process framework that is applicable for all WebApp increments. A *task list* is created by using the generic tasks derived as part of the framework as a starting point and then adapting these by considering the content and functions to be de-rived for a specific WebApp increment.

Each framework action (and its related tasks) can be adapted in one of four ways: (1) a task is applied as is, (2) a task is eliminated because it is not necessary for the increment, (3) a new (custom) task is added, and (4) a task is refined (elaborated) into a number of named subtasks that each becomes part of the schedule.

We noted that the generic design *modeling* action could be accomplished by applying some or all of the following tasks:

- Design the interface.
- Design the aesthetic for the WebApp.
- Design the navigation scheme.
- Design the WebApp architecture.
- Design the content and the structure that supports it.
- Design functional components.
- Select appropriate design patterns.
- Design appropriate security and privacy mechanisms.
- Review the design.

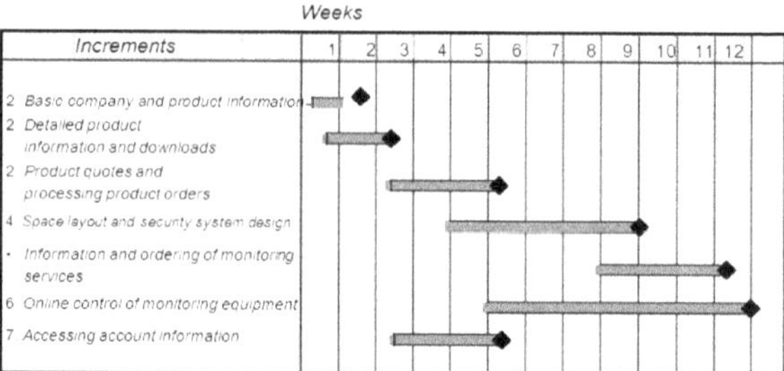

Figure 7.3: Time Line for Macroscopic Project Schedule

As an example, consider the generic task *Design the interface* as it is applied to the fourth increment of SafeHomeAssured.com. Recall that the fourth increment implements the content and function for describing the living or business space to be secured by the *SafeHome* security system. Referring to Figure 7.3, the fourth increment commences at the beginning of the fifth week and terminates at the end of the ninth week.

There is little question that the *Design the interface* task must be conducted. The team recognizes that the interface design is pivotal to the success of the increment and decides to refi ne (elaborate) the task. The following subtasks are derived for the *Design the interface* task for the fourth increment:

- Develop a sketch of the page layout for the space design page.
- Review the layout with stakeholders.
- Design the space layout navigation mechanisms.
- Design the "drawing board" layout.
- Develop procedural details for the graphical wall layout function.
- Develop procedural details for the wall length computation and display function.
- Develop procedural details for the graphical window layout function.
- Develop procedural details for the graphical door layout function.
- Design mechanisms for selecting security system components (sensors, cameras, microphones, etc.).
- Develop procedural details for the graphical layout of security system components.
- Conduct pair walkthroughs as required.

These tasks become part of the increment schedule for the fourth WebApp increment and are allocated over the increment development schedule. They can be input to scheduling software (e.g., Microsoft Project) and used for tracking and control.

7.5.3. How Do We Estimate Effort and Time?

The focus of estimation for most WebE projects is on macroscopic, rather than microscopic, issues. The WebE team assesses whether a planned WebApp increment can be developed with available resources according to defined schedule constraints. This is accomplished by considering each increment's content and function as a whole. In essence, members of the WebE team ask, "Can we deploy the fourth SafeHomeAssured.com increment with three people working for 5 weeks, given our current understanding of the increment, the risks that we've identified, and the task list that we've defined for the work?"

If the team answers "yes," unanimously and without hesitation, no further estimation activities are required. On the other hand, if the team has trepidation about a delivery date that was forced on them by one or more stakeholders, two options are available: (1) voice your concerns but proceed anyway, or (2) do a small amount of detailed estimation in an effort to help yourselves and your stakeholders better understand the resources and time required.

There are two viable (and quick) approaches to detailed estimation for WebApps. The first, *usage scenario–based estimation,* examines the usage scenarios (e.g., use cases) defined for the increment to be built. Examining the team's past history, you establish a value E_{avg}, which is the average effort (in person-days) required to deploy a usage scenario. To estimate the increment, count the number of usage scenarios and multiply by E_{avg}. The number can be adjusted based on the perceived complexity of the usage scenarios. Once the effort is determined, it can be distributed across WebE actions and tasks along the project time line. Finally, the estimates can be used to assess the validity of the deployment dates for the increment. Figure 7.4 illustrates this approach for the fourth SafeHomeAssured.com increment, where the past history for the team indicates that E_{avg} 5 14 person-days. Both usage scenarios to be implemented are considerably more complex than average with complexity multipliers of 2.5 and 2.0, respectively. Hence, the overall ef-fort required to implement the fourth increment is estimated to be 63 person-days to be distributed over a delivery period of 5 weeks.

Usage Scenario	E_{avg}	Complexity	Effort
Develop a layout for the space to be monitored	14	2.5	35
Get recommendations for sensor layout for my space	14	2.0	28
Totals			63

Figure 7.4: Usage Scenario– Based Estimation

It's time for a word of caution. Inexperienced teams (and team leaders) assume a linear relationship exists between people, effort, and time. That is, if 63 person-days are required to model, construct, and deploy an increment, the work could be accomplished by one person working for 63 days, two people working for 32 days, three people working for 21 days, and so forth. Sadly, a linear relationship does not exist. In reality, as more people become involved in a project, more effort is spent on communicating and coordinating (meetings, e-mail, etc.). Additional time is spent on things that have nothing to do with the project (e.g., telephone calls, coordinating the softball league), administrative issues (e.g., applying for a new health insurance plan), and other "nonproductive" work. As a consequence, it may take three people 25 or more calendar days to achieve 63 person-days of effort.

Content and functions	Analysis	Design	Coding	Testing	Delivery	Feed-back	Total
Walls, doorways, windows	1	2	2	2	0.5	0.25	7.75
Sensors	0.5	1.5	1	1	0.25	0.25	4.5
Specify and draw walls, doorways, windows	1.25	3	3	3	1	0.25	11.5
Compute room size	0.5	1	2	1	0.5	0.25	5.25
Save/retrieve named space	0	1	1	0.5	0.5	0.25	3.25
Update/delete named space	0	1	1	0.5	0.5	0.25	3.25
Print named space	0	1	1	0.5	0.5	0.25	3.25
Recommend security hardware	0.5	3	2	2	0.5	0.25	8.25
Specify security hardware	0.5	2	2	3	0.5	0.25	8.25
Totals	4.25	15.5	15	13.5	4.75	2.25	55.25

Figure 7.5: Product-Process Table for Estimation

A second estimation approach uses a *product-process table.* In this approach, all major WebE actions are listed in the first column of the table. All major content objects and functions for an increment are listed in the first row. Team members estimate the amount of effort (in person-days) required to perform the WebE action for each content object and function. Figure 7.5 illustrates this estimation approach for the fourth SafeHomeAssured.com increment. This effort appears to be a bit more optimistic than scenario-based estimates. Both must be reconciled to provide a single estimate. The relatively complex content and functionality of increment 4 demands considerably more WebE effort than earlier increments.

7.5.4. How Do We Represent Task Interdependencies?

Some WebE tasks or actions cannot commence until the work product produced by another is available. Other tasks or actions can occur independently. Therefore, it should come as no surprise that individual WebE tasks have interdependencies based on their sequence.

When more than one person is involved in a WebE project, it is likely that development actions and tasks will be performed in parallel. When this occurs, con-current tasks must be coordinated so that they will be complete when later tasks that require their work product(s) need to be performed.

A *task network,* also called an *activity network,* is a graphic representation of the task flow for a project. It is sometimes used as the mechanism through which task sequence and dependencies are input to an automated project scheduling tool. In its simplest form (used when creating a macroscopic schedule), the task network depicts the overall flow of Web engineering tasks. Figure 7.6 shows a schematic task network for the fourth SafeHome Assured.com increment.

The concurrent nature of WebE actions and tasks leads to a number of important scheduling requirements. Because parallel tasks occur asynchronously, the team leader must determine intertask dependencies to ensure continuous progress toward completion of the increment. In addition, the team leader should be aware of those tasks that lie on the *critical path,* that is, tasks that must be completed on schedule if the increment as a whole is to be completed on schedule.

7.6.   Managing Quality

A WebApp increment is modeled, constructed, and deployed over a relatively short time span. Once it is released to end users, the WebApp increment is exercised and feedback is provided to the WebE team. The feedback provides a reasonably good indication of what works and what doesn't. It is tempting, therefore, to postpone any consideration of WebApp quality until after an increment is deployed, fixing problems when they're pointed out during the first days of usage. There are, of course, a number of flaws in this approach:

Quality problems found by end users are almost always much more expensive to correct than they would have been had they been uncovered earlier in the WebE process flow. Fixing a design error before the WebApp is constructed can be many times less expensive (in expended effort) than trying to correct a deployed WebApp.

Every problem uncovered by end users demands rework, and rework absorbs resources (people and effort) that would have been applied to the next increment. The overall project falls behind schedule. Early users may not fully exercise the increment, leaving content and function untouched. Quality problems may exist in these untouched areas. They will be discovered later (and if you believe Murphy's law) at the worst possible time.

It is therefore advisable for every WebE team to focus on WebApp quality as increments are being engineered. But where do you focus.

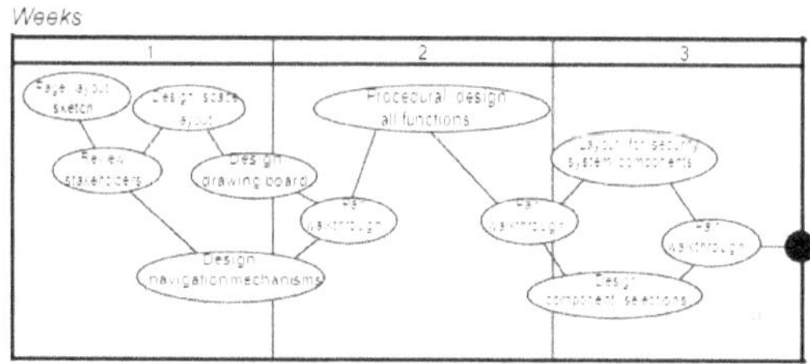

Figure 7.6: A Task Network for the Fourth Increment

7.6.1. *What Quality Assurance Mechanisms Can the Team Use?*

Although quality problems can arise from a variety of sources, their origins can often be traced to a failure to understand or achieve the needs of end users. Therefore, the first quality assurance mechanism for Web engineering is a thoughtful, thorough communication activity. If care is taken as requirements gathering is conducted, then there will be less likelihood that errors. Inconsistencies or omissions will not be passed into subsequent framework activities. The *pair walkthrough* (discussed next) can be used to assess the quality of all work products developed as part of communication. In this case, the walkthrough participants include a Web engineer and one or more stakeholders.

Once requirements for content, function, constraints, and performance are passed forward to the modeling activity, analysis and design tasks commence. In every case, analysis and design models should be assessed for quality. At a minimum, the WebE team can create a generic checklist that you can use to assess the model. For more complex or critical models, a pair walkthrough can be conducted for each model that is created.

Once the WebApp increment code has been generated, a systematic sequence of tests can be initiated to assess the quality of the increment. It is important to note that tests must exercise all user requirements and at the same time examine technical aspects of the increment (e.g., architectural integrity, the correctness of a functional component or content object, and the validity of all links and navigation mechanisms).

The results of all quality assurance mechanisms should be recorded. This will assist the team when changes must be made and will also help the team to correct process weaknesses that led to a class of errors.

7.6.2. *What Are the Mechanics of a Pair Walkthrough?*

Earlier in this chapter, we noted that a pair walkthrough was an effective and agile mechanism for ensuring the quality of work products (e.g., analysis and design models, HTML or XML code, various scripts, and content and functions) that are produced as a consequence of WebE activities.

As an example of the mechanics of a pair walkthrough, we'll consider a portion of the analysis model of the fourth increment of the SafeHomeAssured.com WebApp. This increment implements a layout for the space to be monitored and recommends sensors for that space.

A member of the WebE team, working in conjunction with a specific stake-holder from the marketing department,[11] produces a portion of the analysis model (in this case, a graphical description of the user interface for implementing a space layout). As the interface model is developed, the Web engineer works together with a knowledgeable stakeholder (a marketing person who can play the role of an end user) and conducts an ongoing pair walkthrough. Both the Web engineer and the stakeholder review the interface model as it evolves, addressing questions such as:

- Is there anything about the page layout that is problematic?
- Are menu items meaningful, complete, and intuitive?
- Is the space layout scheme easy to use? Intuitive?
- Can you envision how you'd navigate to this page and from it to other functionality and content?
- Have we missed any key functionality or content on this page?
- What are you assuming about this model?

These and other questions are addressed repeatedly as the model evolves. The result is ongoing corrections and/or modifications to the model.

7.6.3. *What Are the Mechanics of a Team Walkthrough?*

There are situations in which the entire WebE team will review a work product. This situation occurs when the work product (e.g., a navigation design) may have broad impact for the entire WebApp, and hence it is important that everyone under-stands the issues and has input into the review.

Two team members use the "pair programming" approach to develop some aspect of the WebApp. Once they are convinced that the work product is complete in draft form, the pair (called the *producers* of the work product) asks other members of the team to participate in a *team walkthrough.* The producers give the other re-viewers any information that has been produced (either in hard copy form, if feasible, or in electronic form). The reviewers promise to spend at least 30 to 45 minutes reviewing the work product and listing any issues, problems, or impressions based on the review.

Within 24 hours (preferably sooner), a team walkthrough begins. The producers of the work product begin by "walking through" the work product, explaining what it represents and how the reader might interpret what is shown. As this occurs, the reviewers ask questions (often based on notes developed before the review) and point out potential problem areas. The producers note each of these without trying to solve them immediately. As the walkthrough proceeds, the participants follow these guidelines:

- **Review the product, not the producer.** Conducted properly, the team walkthrough should leave all participants with a warm feeling of accomplishment. Conducted improperly, the walkthrough can take on the aura of an inquisition. Errors should be pointed out gently; the tone of the walk-through should be loose and constructive; the intent should not be to embarrass or belittle, but rather to assist.
- **Set an agenda and maintain it.** One of the key maladies of meetings of all types is drift. A walkthrough should be kept on track and on schedule.
- **Limit debate and rebuttal.** When an issue is raised by a reviewer, there may not be agreement on its impact. Rather than spending time debating the question, the issue should be recorded for resolution later.
- **Enunciate problem areas, but don't attempt to solve every problem noted.** A walkthrough is not a problem-solving session.
- **Take written notes.** Notes may be entered directly into a notebook computer.
- **Spend enough time to uncover quality problems, but not one minute more.** In general, a team walkthrough should be completed within 60 to 90 minutes at the most.

As an example of a situation in which a team walkthrough is required, the entire WebE team might decide to review aspects of the design model to help ensure that errors, inconsistencies, and omissions are uncovered before code generation commences prior to beginning the construction activity for the fourth SafeHome Assured. com increment.

7.6.4. *Do Criteria for Quality Exist for WebApps?*

Even the best walkthroughs won't work if the people looking at the WebE work product don't know what to look for. The sidebar contains a comprehensive set of online resources [Qui01] that provide quality criteria and guidelines for WebApps.

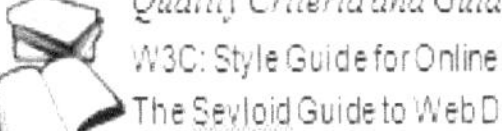

Quality Criteria and Guidelines for WebApps

W3C: Style Guide for Online Hypertext	www.w3.org/Provider/Style
The Sevloid Guide to Web Design	www.sev.com.au/webzone/design/guide.asp
Web Pages That Suck	www.webpagesthatsuck.com/index.html
Resources on Web Style	www.westegg.com/unmaintained/badpages
Gartner's Web Evaluation Tool	www.gartner.com/ebusiness/website-ings
IBM Corp: Web Guidelines	www-3.ibm.com/ibm/easy/eou_ext.nsf/ Publish/572
World Wide Web Usability	http://ijhcs.open.ac.uk
Interface Hall of Shame	www.iarchitect.com/mshame.htm
Art and the Zen of Web Sites	www.tlc-systems.com/webtips.shtml
Designing for the Web: Empirical Studies	www.microsoft.com/usability/webconf.htm
Nielsen's useit.com	www.useit.com
Quality of Experience	www.qualityofexperience.org
SAP Design Guide	www.sapdesignguild.org
Creating Killer Web Sites	www.killersites.com/core.html
All Things at Web	www.pantos.org/atw
SUN's New Web Design	www.sun.com/980113/sunonnet
Tognazzini, Bruce: Homepage	www.asktog.com
Webmonkey	http://hotwired.lycos.com/webmonkey/ design/?tw=design
World's Best Websites	www.worldbestwebsites.com
Yale University: Yale Web Style Guide	http://info.med.yale.edu/caim/manual

7.7.   Managing Change

Because an incremental process flow is used for Web engineering, it's relatively easy to manage change *if* you and other stakeholders have discipline and patience. Because the development time for an increment is short, it is often possible to delay the introduction of requested changes until the next increment, thereby reducing the disruptive effects associated with changes that must be implemented on the fly.

However, this strategy implies a subtle change in our approach to each increment. Not only does the *n* 1 1st WebApp increment implement content and functionality associated with the increment, but it may also incorporate changes to content and functionality requested for the *n*th increment (changes that have been delayed until after the *n*th increment is initially deployed). Of course, this is only reasonable if none of those extra changes are "showstoppers"; that is, if the delivered increment (without the changes to be included in the next increment) is still an acceptable solution.

7.7.1. How Should Criticality and Impact of a Change Be Assessed?

In order to assess the criticality and impact of any requested change, each change should be categorized into one of four classes:

- **Class 1.** Content or function change that corrects a minor error or enhances local content or functionality
- **Class 2**. Content or function change that has an impact on other content objects or functional components within the increment
- **Class 3.** Content of function change that has a broad impact across a WebApp (e.g., major extension of functionality, significant enhancement or reduction in content, major required changes in navigation)
- **Class 4.** Major design change (e.g., a change in interface design or navigation approach) that will be immediately noticeable to one or more categories of end users.

Once the requested change has been categorized, it can be assessed according to the algorithm shown in Figure 7.7.

Referring to the figure, class 1 and 2 changes are treated informally and are handled in an agile manner. For a class 1 change, a Web engineer evaluates the impact of the change, but no external review or documentation is required. As the change is made, standard check-in and check-out procedures are enforced by con-figuration repository tools. For class 2 changes, it is incumbent on the Web engineer to review the impact of the change on related objects (or to ask other developers responsible for those objects to do so). If the change can be made without requiring significant changes to other objects, modification occurs without additional review or documentation. If substantive changes are required, further evaluation and planning are necessary. Class 3 and 4 changes are also treated in an agile manner, but some descriptive documentation and more formal review procedures are required. A *change description* describing the change and providing a brief assessment of the impact of the change is developed for class 3 changes.

The description is distributed to all members of the Web engineering team (including other stakeholders who have interest) who review it to better assess its impact. A change description is also developed for class 4 changes, but in this case, the review is conducted by all stakeholders.

7.7.2. When Do We Delay Making the Change?

As we noted in the introduction to this section, changes tend to disrupt work and delay the deployment of a WebApp increment. The reason for this is obvious— people who are working on content or functionality associated with an increment must stop what they're doing and address the change. This takes time.

In order to avoid a disruption to the increment work schedule, a change associated with increment n should deployed. That is, changes are "locked out" of the increment while it is undergoing development. The requested changes must, of course, be evaluated and incorporated into the increment, but only after the increment has been delivered for the first time. At this point you may be thinking: "My stakeholders won't put up with that approach. They request a change and want it implemented immediately." We've encountered the same situation, but that doesn't mean that the "make the change now!" culture can't be changed. In order to change this culture, stake-holders must understand that changes are *not* free—they absorb resources and they take time. Therefore, the stakeholder is always left with a trade-off—work can be interrupted and changes can be made, but delivery dates will slip and costs will invariably escalate. In most situations, it is better to delay the implementation of a change until it can be accomplished in the least disruptive (and therefore, least costly and time consuming) manner.

There are situations, however, where a change should be made immediately. The change should be made immediately, if:

- Delaying the change will result in more work than making it on the spot.
- The usability of the increment by end users will be severely degraded with-out the change.
- Significant monetary damages will occur if the change is not made immediately.
- Regulatory or legal requirements demand that the deployment include the change.
- If one or more of these criteria are met, you must make the change as part of the current increment.

7.7.3. *Should Changes Be Made to All Related Work Products?*

Work products produced during the WebE process serve one of two purposes:

1. They can be an informal record of information gathered during a WebE activity (e.g., a list of content and functional requirements gathered during the communication activity), or
2. They can be a representation (model) of the WebApp that is used to guide subsequent WebE activities (e.g., an interface design model that will guide the coding of the interface during construction).

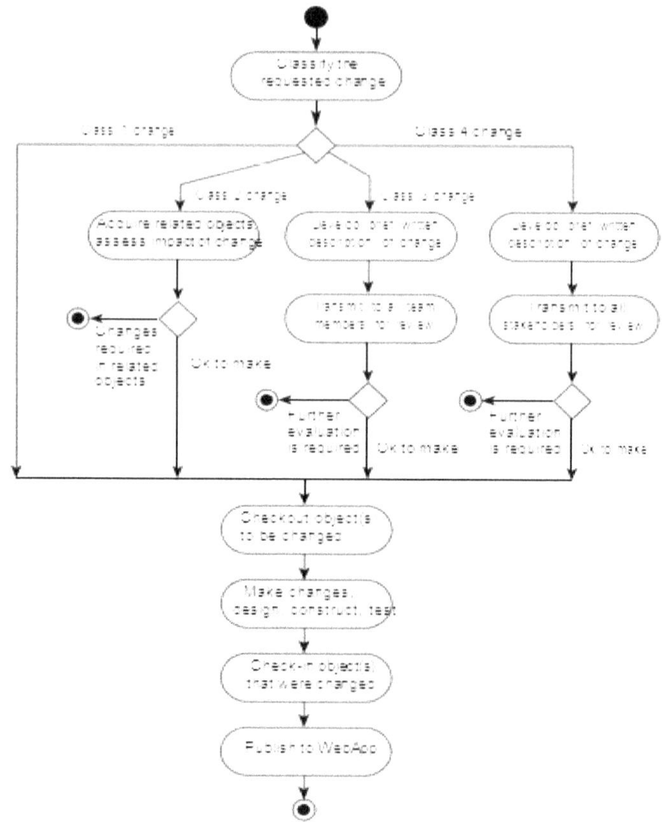

Figure 7.7: Managing Changes for WebApps

As a general rule of thumb, work products that fall into the first category need not be updated as changes are requested and made. However, work products in the second category should be modified to reflect any changes so that they remain useful in subsequent WebE activities. It's important to note, however, that keeping *all* work products in the second category (e.g., design models) up to date can be burdensome for a WebE team. How then does the WebE team choose the work products that should be updated as changes are made?

A pragmatic approach is to answer this question: "What aspects of the design can be better represented as an executable implemention?" In some instances, the only permanent description of some aspect of the WebApp is the WebApp itself. For example, once the interface design model has been implemented in HTML, there is little reason to maintain the actual design model of the interface. Changes to the interface will be guided by the implementation, not the model. Hence, the model can be archived (for historical purposes), but need not be kept up to date. On the other hand, a design model of a complex function might be useful even after the function has been implemented and deployed. The reason for this is that the model is represented at a higher level of abstraction and will facilitate understanding by people who have not been involved in the original implementation. In this case, the functional model should be updated as changes are made to the function.

7.8.   Tracking the Project

For a WebE project, on-time deployment of a WebApp increment is often the primary measure of overall progress. But before the increment is available, a Web engineer will inevitably encounter the question, "Where are we?"

To provide an answer to this question, you'll need to track progress as a WebApp increment is being developed. But how? For small and moderately sized Web engineering projects, an increment may be developed over a period of only 2 or 3 weeks. At best, intermediate milestones are informally defined, and the project schedule may not have been developed at a granularity that will aid in tracking.

7.8.1.   *Are There Any Macroscopic Indicators of Progress Problems?*

At a macroscopic level, there are signs indicating that an increment (or the entire project) is in trouble. John Reel [Ree99] suggests 10 signs that indicate that an information systems project is in jeopardy. We have adapted these for Web Apps:

- The WebE team doesn't understand its customer's needs.
- The WebApp scope is poorly defined.
- Changes are managed poorly.
- The chosen technology changes.
- Business needs appear to be changing (or are ill defi ned).
- Deadlines are unrealistic.
- Users are not really interested in the WebApp.
- Sponsorship is lost (or was never properly obtained).
- The WebE team lacks people with appropriate skills.
- Practitioners avoid best practices and lessons learned.

Throughout this and earlier chapters, we've discussed a WebE process that can help eliminate these problems. Take the process seriously and you'll avoid what some jaded industry professionals call the "90-90 rule." The first 90 percent of a system absorbs 90 percent of the allotted effort and time. The last 10 percent takes the other 90 percent of the allotted effort and time [Zah94]. The seeds that lead to the 90-90 rule are contained in the macroscopic indicators noted in the preceding list.

7.8.2.   *What Criteria Are Used to Track Progress?*

One way to track progress as a WebApp increment is being developed is to poll the WebE team to determine which framework activities have been completed. How-ever, this approach can be unreliable because completion of a framework activity is an indication of progress only if appropriate[12] work products have been developed.

Another approach is to determine how many user scenarios have been implemented and how many user scenarios (for a given increment) remain to be implemented. This provides a rough indication of the relative degree of "completeness" of the project increment.

If the WebE team has taken the time to construct a detailed work schedule for the increment, progress can be tracked by determining how many work tasks have been completed, how many work products have been produced and reviewed, and how much confidence individual team members have in the increment completion date.

References

1. G. Kappel, B. Proll, S. Reich and W. Retschitzegger, Web Engineering: The Discipline of Systematic Development of Web Applications, John Wiley and Sons Ltd, ISBN: 9780470064894.
2. R.S. Pressman and D. Lowe, Web Engineering: A Practitioner's Approach, 1st Edition, Tata Macgraw Hill Publications, ISBN 9780073523293.
3. L. Shklar and R. Rosen, Web Application Architecture: Principles, Protocols and Practices, 2nd Edition, Wiley, ISBN: 047051860X.
4. G.W Leeky-Thompson, Just Enough Web Programming with XHTML, PHP, and MySQL, 1st Edition, Cenagage Learning, ISBN: 159863481X.
5. A. Moller and M. Schwartzbach, An Introduction to XML and Web Technologies, 1st Edition, Pearson Education, New Delhi, 2009.
6. C. Bates, Web Programming: Building Internet Applications, 3rd Edition, Wiley India Edition, ISBN: 8126512903.

D91667

Name...........................

Reg .No.........................

Third Semester M.Sc. Degree Examination, December 2015

(CUCSS)

Computer Science

CSS 3E 05F-Web Engineering

(2014 Admissions)

Time: Three Hours   Maximum Weightage: 36

Part A

Answer All Questions

Each Question Carries 1 Weightage

1. Define Web Engineering.

2. What is tracking?

3. What do we mean by requirement specification in Web Engineering?

4. What is architecture?

5. What is stress testing?

6. What is functional design?

7. What are the test objectives in Web Engineering?

8. What is software quality?

9. Distinguish between testing and debugging?

10. What is modeling?

11. What are reuse?

12. What is mean by formal technical review?

(12×1 = 12 weightage)

Part B

Answer Any Six Questions

Each Question Carries 2 Weightage

1. Explain the characteristics of Web Engineering?

2. Explain the principles of requirement engineering for web application.

3. Write a short note on risk management.

4. Briefly explain text modeling?

5. Describe quality assurance in detail.

6. Differentiate browser testing and usability testing.

7. Briefly explain different test levels.

8. Write short note on evolution of Web Engineering

9. Briefly explain presentation modeling.

(6×2 = 12 weightage)

Part C

Answer any Three Questions

Each question carries 4 weightage

1. Explain modeling requirement.

2. Explain quality management in web application.

3. Explain basic components of web application architecture.

4. Explain load, stress and continuous testing.

5. Explain the activities involved in risk management.

6. What are the different steps in interface design process?

(3×4 = 12 weightage)